THE **MYSTERY**
OF **DEATH**

DOROTHEE SOELLE

**Translated by Nancy Lukens-Rumscheidt
and Martin Lukens-Rumscheidt**

**Fortress Press
Minneapolis**

THE MYSTERY OF DEATH

Cover design by John Goodman
Book design by Douglas Schmitz

Library of Congress Cataloging-in-Publication Data
Sölle, Dorothee.
 [Mystik des Todes. English]
 The mystery of death / Dorothee Sölle (1929–2003); translated by
Nancy and Martin Lukens-Rumscheidt.
     p. cm.
 Includes bibliographical references.
 ISBN 978-0-8006-3891-7 (hardcover : alk. paper)
 1. Death—Religious aspects—Christianity. I. Title.
BT825.S673 2007
236'.1—dc22   2006100714

The paper used in this publication meets the minimum requirements of American National Standard for Information Sciences—Permanence of Paper for Printed Library Materials, ANSI Z329.48-1984.

Manufactured in the U.S.A.

11   10   09   08   07   1   2   3   4   5   6   7   8   9   10

I dedicate this book to two people whom I love and respect, who understand the art of healing:

Dr. Wulf Nachtwey, Hamburg,
and
Dr. Caroline Soelle de Hilari, La Paz, Bolivia

Steh nicht an meinem Grab und
weine

Ich bin nicht dort, ich schlafe nicht

Ich bin die tausend Winde die blasen

Ich bin der Glanz des Diamanten
im Schnee

ich bin das Sonnenlicht auf den
reifen Ähren

Ich bin der sanfte Regen.

Wenn du erwachst in Morgenstille

Ich bin das rauscht sich Aden der Ruhe

von ruhigen Vögeln in kreisendem

Ich bin die sanften Sterne die nachts
scheinen

Steh nicht an meinem Grab + weine

Ich bin nicht dort, ich bin nicht gestorben

Written on April 24, 2003, in Hamburg.[1]

contents

f o r e w o r d

---

by Fulbert Steffensky

IN 1997 DOROTHEE SOELLE COMPLETED *Mystik und Widerstand*,[1] to her the most important and favorite among her books. It was very difficult for her to let the manuscript go at that time. She found it lacked one chapter: "The Mysticism of Death." Her many lectures and reading tours prevented her from continuing with the project for some time. A few years later, however, she took up this theme again and worked on it up to the last days of her life. She wrote the last few lines two days before her death.

This is the book of a person who has grown tired. Writing came easily to her throughout her life. With this book she struggled over every line. She tormented herself, but not only in the way one torments oneself over a book. It was a confrontation with finitude and with death; it was her preparation for death. The book is a fragment, as any human life is a fragment. Should one publish a fragment? Our family thought about this for a long time, and one of our arguments for publishing it was that she intended to do so. Out of respect for her we made no changes except to correct a few typographical errors. It should be published just as it was when she wrote her last sentence—conceptually incomplete, unsystematic with citations. We did not even delete redundancies, preferring to avoid any attitude of superiority toward the dead.

There was another reason we opted to publish the text as it is. After Dorothee Soelle's death we received hundreds of letters in which people wrote that it was through her influence that they had found their way to the church, remained in the church, studied theology, or found courage for a pastoral vocation. We believe these people deserve to experience the intimacy of an incomplete text and its unprotected thoughts. Many of them expressly requested that the book be published. After all, she spoke often and in many contexts about her project. Now, it is as if she had just gotten up from her desk for a moment and would be back shortly to continue writing. (Perhaps it is really so!) Whoever reads this book will sense that her hand became tired. What never became tired is her wonderful, enraged passion for life.

Translators' Preface

As Dorothee Soelle's widower, Fulbert Steffensky, stated, his intention in publishing Dorothee Soelle's incomplete manuscript was to preserve her final works in the fragmentary form in which they existed when she died on April 27, 2003. We expect that Soelle's English-speaking audience will also be interested to know how her thinking was evolving at the time of her death as she wrote what she considered the "missing chapter" to her major *oeuvre*, *The Silent Cry: Mysticism and Resistance*. We thus followed Fulbert Steffensky's example in avoiding extensive editing or deletion of redundancies. At the same time we have attempted to make the German text accessible to our readers by providing endnotes by chapter (beginning on p. 137) to clarify allusions or peculiarities of usage and to refer the reader to sources where Soelle provided incomplete references or none at all.

The same applies to the additional essay included as chapter 5 of this volume, "Where Love Is, There Is God," a meditation by Soelle in texts and images that appeared separately in German in 2004.[1]

We have rendered all references to and quotations from Scripture according to the New Revised Standard Version (NRSV), unless otherwise noted, adding literal translations of the German version of the Bible used by Soelle if its wording differs significantly from the NRSV and is important to understanding her reading of the passage.

Translations of hymns cited in the text from the German Protestant hymnal, the *Evangelisches Gesangbuch* (*EGB*), many of which are poetic and religious classics, are our own unless otherwise indicated. We have followed Soelle's practice of citing the *EGB* hymn number in parentheses in the body of the text.

Translations of original poems by Dorothee Soelle are our own unless otherwise credited. Some of these have not, to our knowledge, been published in either German or English until now; others are translated from German published originals, the titles of which are provided in the notes to the sections in which they appear.

In the case of Soelle's extensive allusions to and quotations from poems, essays, and philosophical or theological texts that exist in English translation, we have reproduced and credited those published translations if they are readily available and if we find they accurately represent Soelle's intent in citing them (see "Works Cited," p. 133). Otherwise we provide our own translations. Often, in attempting to integrate the equivalent lines from a published English version of a quoted poem into Soelle's prose, we found it necessary to remain closer to the German original than existing versions. These are nevertheless referenced in our translators' notes.

Soelle's interpretations of poetry and other literature that she integrates into her meditation on death, often quoting long passages at a time, are of course based on German originals or German translations of originals in other languages. In order to get at the layers of the poet Soelle's strikingly original and reflective use of language, we have translated certain key words in various ways, depending on the context. In many cases, we chose to paraphrase for lack of a single word that does justice to her creative images and concepts.

Soelle uses a number of more or less untranslatable German plays on words that are central to her writing on the significance of Western industrialized culture's attitudes and practices surrounding death and dying. She elaborates on how these attitudes are reflected in our use of language. For example, in her discussion entitled "The Denial of Limits," we find a series of terms containing the root word *Grenze* (limit, boundary, border), which Soelle has culled from everyday usage and developed into an analysis of the relationship between linguistic habits and deeper cultural values: *Ausgrenzen* (to discriminate or marginalize, typically on the basis of nationality, gender, race, or social status); *Begrenzen* (to limit, as in growth, consumption, and so on); and *Ent-*

grenzen (to abolish or eliminate boundaries). Further examples are the term *Herrschaft* (dominion, dominance, sovereign rule or reign, government), which has occupied feminists, especially feminist theologians, concerned with issues of patriarchy; the term *Reich* (realm, empire); and the term *Heimat* (home, homeland, home town or country, place of origin). From these latter contexts arises Soelle's reflection on *Heimatlosigkeit* (homelessness), that is, not in the sense of lacking shelter, but in the sense of feeling like a stranger in one's own city or country or even in an entire culture. Similarly, we translate the words *Fremd/Fremdheit* (strange, of foreign origin, not from here, different, alien/feeling like an alien) variously because their usage in German carries such different historical and contemporary overtones than the concept of "stranger" in English. Soelle clearly integrates her sense of the spiritual dimensions of language, her "theo-poetics," into her writing, which we have tried to emulate in our translation.

A word about our methods of citation, given the incompleteness of many of Soelle's references: In the case of imprecisely quoted phrases and longer passages from unspecified works of major writers such as Bertolt Brecht, Thomas Hobbes, Martin Luther, Jürgen Moltmann, Rosemary Radford Ruether, Mark Twain, and Albert Schweitzer, translations are our own. Likewise, where Soelle cites articles from current German periodicals, we translate the citation and include her incomplete references in a note. The same goes for incomplete citations from less familiar authors.

This volume is the result of the translators' fruitful collaboration on every part of the book. Nancy Lukens-Rumscheidt translated the foreword by Fulbert Steffensky and chapters 1 and 3, drafted the translators' preface, and compiled the list of works cited. Martin Lukens-Rumscheidt translated chapters 2, 4, and 5. The epilogue was translated collaboratively by Nancy and Martin Lukens-Rumscheidt. We are each responsible for translating the author's notes, indicated by [DS], in the chapters we translated and for locating the English versions of titles cited in those chapters. Nancy Lukens-Rumscheidt translated the eight original Soelle poems contained in this volume and created the translators' endnotes.

Our profound gratitude and admiration are due to Fulbert Steffensky and to the late Dorothee Soelle for their life's work and partnership, and to Michael West of Fortress Press, who recognized the need for Soelle's final works to appear in English.

p r o l o g u e

Dear Mr. Death and Co.

DEAR MR. DEATH,

I do not know your address, but I know that you have an enormous number of employees, service people, and well-paid advisers at your disposal in your successful enterprise. I have a favor to ask you, and it is my wish that you read this message through and pass it along to the appropriate person.

For over thirty years I have lived with the great love of my life. It is not you I am afraid of, Mr. Death; what I fear are all the tubes and pipes in the hospital that try to stave you off or postpone your arrival. I grew up with the "Master from Germany," and I know something about the "black milk of dawn" that is being prepared these days.[1] I am aware that we must dance to your drumbeat, and I, as I struggle on many fronts with your employees, am not afraid. What I fear is being left alone if and when my partner, the one with whom I laugh and cry, must leave me. I am quite sure that if this were the case, I would use all the resources at my disposal to face you. But it would be different if he and I could both walk this road together.

My partner knows that I fear his passing more than my own. He is capable of wishing that he stay a bit longer. I flunk this test. I simply cannot wish for this—and you know, of course, that wishing is another word for praying. Perhaps his love is greater than mine, although I hate to admit it. Sometimes I suspect that love—in case we know what we mean when we utter this word—is the only thing you respect.

This is why I would like to request that you not separate the two of us.

chapter one

Old and New Fears

The Terror of Death

"The terror of death is death itself," says Martin Luther in his *Table Talk*.

"Terror mortis est ipsa mors." The terror of death is death itself and nothing else. I have been reflecting about this sentence in a world in which the word "terror" has been infused with an enormous new energy. It has come to mean horror, dread, *Angst*. It can be associated with an object like execution, or a news item like September 11, 2001, that is, with a particular experience. In my childhood it was used by the Nazis to refer to the bomb attacks against the German population—a usage one can hardly dispute. Terror and death belong in the same phrase. Some of my close friends compared the September 2001

murderers with the Nazi murderers. I could not get my head around that because the Nazis who merely pushed buttons to turn on poison gas did so without feeling any connection between themselves and the terror. Doesn't the expression "suicide bomber" reveal a different relationship with fear, with the terror of death?

Here I would like to relate an experience, not in order to justify the suicide bombers, but to offer some explanation why in some places in the world of abject poverty a certain amount of understanding was expressed for them. My daughter, a medical doctor living in Bolivia, recently told me that one of the most frequent causes of death among adults in the Andean Highlands is suicide. A sixty-four-year-old woman I knew slightly took rat poison, the cheapest way to go. The degree of impoverishment in this region is so great that the younger people in the villages where there was always poverty—but where for centuries people survived on potatoes—are now fleeing to the urban slums, that is, to lives of begging, prostitution, or drug dealing, while the elderly remain in the country and see no purpose in vegetating any further. The fear of lost relationships that comes with death is already death. *Terror mortis est ipsa mors*—the fear of death is death itself and nothing else.

But is this true for all time? And for everyone? Is death the all-defining terrorist? The epoch characterized by this kind of fear dawned already centuries ago. A writer as late as Thomas Hobbes (1588–1679), who used the "war of everyone against everyone" to explain the natural world, sees the fear of death as the cause of war. He calls life "nasty, brutish, and short"—and adds that the worst thing about life is the constant fear and danger of violent death. This *terror mortis*, which, according to Luther, surrounds us with death in the midst of life, has become more and more unknown in the affluent world. Perhaps we have quite different fears today.

Luther's 1519 "Sermon on Preparing to Die," also contained in his *Death and Immortality*, is a text that instructs people how they can become free of the terror of death. Fears are one of the Devil's best means to turn humans so completely in on themselves that they seem almost doubled over; never are people so self-involved as when they fear death. The terror-driven images and dreams, such as that of suffocating, are fantasies in which people desperately cling to life and precisely in so doing forget God. One of the great teachings of the mystics is that remembering God is the way in which we forget ourselves and can become free of ourselves.[1] Those who cannot forget themselves can no longer notice that they have long since forgotten God. Forgetting God and forgetting oneself are mutually exclusive. They are an either-or. For Luther it is the Devil "who drives stupid human nature to the fear of death, to love and to the cares of life, whereby human beings, weighed down with such thoughts, forget God. . . . For the more deeply death is considered, regarded and recognized, the more difficult and dangerous dying becomes."[2]

The human being turned in on him- or herself, the *homo incurvatus in se*, is the very definition of the sinner in Luther's commentary on Paul's Letter to the Romans. In the fear of death God is quite naturally forgotten, and that is exactly what the Devil wants to achieve. "Then the Devil will have a ball."[3] Our fears turn us in onto our own ego. Not only the feelings of guilt that overcome many people in their fear of death do this; other forms of "cares, grief, and personal woes" can also hold us hostage and take complete control over us. We only become free in looking away from ourselves, which always means also leaving one's present situation. "I was completely transported when I heard the third movement of the cello concerto" is an everyday expression used by people not turned in on themselves. They stand upright and reach out beyond themselves. I am not only I.

However, self-reflection does not lead us to achieve this liberation from the delusion of self. Indeed, Luther's hymn says quite precisely what self-reflection does achieve (*EGB* 341, vv. 2–3):

> *And so I fell in deep despair,*
> *My life held naught of Good,*
> *Fear drove me to abandon Hope,*
> *So naught was left for me but Death,*
> *To Hell I must descend.*

Moving out of ego-imprisonment requires other images than those of death and hell. In another context Luther notes in his wonderful pastoral thoughtfulness, "For this we need a bright, clear saying from

Scripture on which to ground ourselves." A more recent reflection of this is found in H. M. Gutmann's *Mit den Toten Leben: Eine evangelische Perspektive* (*Living with the Dead: A Protestant Perspective*).[4] We cannot manage this alone; we need nudges that chase away our destructive fixation on ourselves and invite us to perceive the other, the not-I.

As Luther lay dying, he prayed from Psalm 68:21: "Thou, O God, art Lord, in the midst of death."[5] Becoming one with God wipes out the fear of death. The person who stands in relationship with God is drawn out of his or her self. As many examples from clinical ministry testify, one can even escape from oneself as a dying person. A child dying of leukemia said to his parents, "You can't come yet; I'm going ahead." The child had mercifully been lifted beyond the self. Such is the way of being free from *terror mortis*.

La danse macabre—the Dance of Death

What did these old fears look like? Can we even begin to appreciate what they felt like? The reality of fourteenth- and fifteenth-century life is characterized by great famine, leprosy, and the plague. In Genoa, where the plague first broke out in 1350, every third person died of it. The many "dances of death" that originated in those days point to the inevitability of death in infinitely varied forms of derision, revenge, and despair. At first these were rhymed texts, but early on they were elaborately illustrated and thus became very popular. They contained two different elements. One was the traditional repentance sermon, the *memento mori*, the reminder of my death, the judgment, the night that is part of life's day and is conjured up again and again in the Psalms: "Lord, let me know my end, and what is the measure of my days; let me know how fleeting my life is" (Ps 39:4). The other, presumably older element is the dance itself and its many diverse performative aspects. In African and Asian cultures there are dances that the living perform for the dead; they express their grief through the movement of dancing. In 1994 when an African woman was buried in Aachen, Germany, her funeral procession took the form of a celebratory dance in which the coffin was thrown into the air several times. What does it mean to dance for the dead? Does it please them? Is it like giving someone flowers? Is it a way of overcoming the fear of death that is being expressed in such a culture? Is there a way in which the living and the dead belong together, and we have just lost touch with this?

The late medieval *danse macabre*, as it was called in Paris in 1425, was not a dance for the dead, but a dance against the living, performed by none other than Death himself. The many kinds of dances document the power of Death. The great Equalizer likes to appear with elegant bows and movements, often equipped with numerous lovely musical instruments. In Albrecht Dürer's "Knight, Death, and the Devil," Death, the King, rides wearing a crown, but otherwise he is a wretched heap of bones on a noble steed.

He apparently wants to entice and attract people of every age and status, whether nun or little girl, emperor or pope, small child or old man, plowman or scholar, beggar or prince.

A late medieval mnemonic poem warns:[6]

Come, mortals, meet your fate,
The hourglass is spent.
From men of high estate
To peasants stooped and bent.

For wagers no more chance,
Do not complain nor swoon;
Now you must dance the dance
And I will name the tune.

The word "wagers" here suggests haggling or negotiating in order to bribe Death with money or goods, youth or beauty, and thus gain a "stay of execution." All these efforts are useless in the face of Death's claim. The dance is danced, no matter how much the dance partners might resist. It may be that we all fail to hear the tune that Death plays. But Death keeps on playing. It is characteristic of the dances of death that the tragic and the comic intermingle. Mockery is an essential ingredient; often it expresses the greatest proximity to Resurrection. In Luther's Easter hymn "Christ Lay in Death's Dark Prison," one cannot miss this message:

Scripture this truth doth proclaim:
One Death did another maim;
Death is mocked forever.[7]

What remains is the clear fact that all mortals are equal in face of death.

In feudal society, with its fixed roles according to one's estate, this verse addressed not only mortality but also the equality of all in the face of the "man with the scythe" who cuts them down like grass, flowers, or sheaves of wheat. Dances of death represented the equality of human beings in ever new ways through mockery, slapstick, and biting jokes. One might argue whether it is a "revolutionary" melody that Death plays. Jürgen Moltmann, for one, considers it an equality only in the negative sense, not in the positive; he sees death as an "equalizer in the beyond, not in the here and now."

But I often ask myself whether death is not the very inventor of equality and whether human beings are permitted any equality at all without the consciousness of death's power. As it is repressed in the world of the rich, so too the consciousness of human equality disappears. We all know, and are reminded daily, that there are simply "winners" and "losers." Perhaps the religion of the winners must exclude and repress death as far as possible from their consciousness. Can equality in the negative sense be so neatly distinguished from equality in the positive, revolutionary sense of human rights for all—for example, the right to go to school?

There were many other forms of the dance of death. I will illustrate with a few literary examples. In Goethe's poem on this theme,[8] the dead arise from their graves for an hour at midnight—veiled in white sheets—to dance together in the cemetery.

Here the dance represents an interruption of the state of death, a breaking of life into death. This mingling of the dead and the living has existed in all older cultures that know no concept of "clinically dead." Goethe's tower watchman allows the Devil to talk him into stealing a sheet; the skeleton that is seen with him climbs up the tower after him. The dramatic text closes with the following lines, which suggest even the dead man could die all over again:

> *The bell is heard thundering a mighty "One"*
> *And below the skeleton smashes to bits.*

In a romantic ballad by Heinrich Heine, the abandoned lover Don Ramiro comes to the wedding of Donna Clara, his "long beloved." She had bid him farewell, then politely invited him to her wedding. He comes and dances with her as Death. She asks again and again about his "cloak of midnight blackness," about his snow-white cheeks, about the aroma of corpses emanating from him, and his reply again and again is only the mysterious, "It was you told me to come here!"[9] There are few texts in which the proximity of love and death, even their interchangeability, is described so ingeniously and hair-raisingly.

The Russian writer Maxim Gorky wrote a long poem called "Death and the Maiden."[10] It begins with a confrontation between love and power. The czar rides into a village in a bitter rage "following a serious military defeat." There he hears a young girl laughing in an elderberry tree. In a gruff tone he barks at her, "Don't waste your stupid laughter on me, wench." Her retort is fresh and immediate: "You go away! I'm chatting with my lover. Why don't you go away, Father Czar?" In response the czar orders his entourage to kill her. After this introduction comes a dialogue between the young girl and Death, which ends with Death's invitation to the girl: "Be good, Child, be reasonable, now into your grave!" The young woman sings a song that I would call mystical, invoking praise for love that transports one beyond all fears: "In his arms I feel as if the world no longer existed!" Suddenly Death comes to understand something new, which has been absent in all earlier versions of the *danse macabre*: "You'll never get your hands on her as long as she loves another." After this Death decides to follow on the path of Love. The poem ends with an optimistic philosophical reflection:

> *Since then Love and Death are like*
> *two tender conspirators in life.*
> *They both dance at all celebrations*
> *Whether weddings, births, or funeral feasts.*
> *And slyly see to it that the blessing of this life*
> *Does not depart from human souls.*

This blessing seems to have escaped us contemporaries. Do Death and Love, these tender conspirators, still walk inseparably, hand in hand?

New Fears

My mother died at eighty-seven, and she did not want to live any longer. She had a breakdown a year earlier, was in intensive care, and was fixed up enough to be able to be at home, but she was no longer able to walk down the stairs to the garden. She liked to quote a baroque poem by Duke Anton Ulrich, smiling as she recited the words: "I've now lived long enough; by now it's time to die." On her birthday she called me at an unusually early hour and told me in a voice radiant with happiness that her favorite granddaughter had written to her, "Grandmother, I wish for you that you don't have any more birthdays." "Finally someone understands me!" was her comment. We, her four children, wished this for her, too, but would never have dared say so.[11] As my mother lay dying—she had not spoken for days—our old family physician came to visit and I said to him, "She really should not have to be in pain any longer." He hesitated and then asked me, "Or do you think hospital?" My mother, comatose for days already, was suddenly wide awake and shouted indignantly, "No! Anything but that!" She wanted to go; her greatest fear was having her life extended again.

These are new fears that have grown out of, and are still growing along with, advances in the medical field. The terror of death has in many instances been replaced by the terror of technocracy. The old fears—of starvation, death in childbirth, premature death—are now distant memories. But does this mean we are living freer of fear? The Swedish writer Henning Mankell spends most of his life in Mozambique, Africa, and his experience with old age and death there is completely different than in Sweden. He is fifty-five, and there that means he is among the aged population. The average life expectancy in Mozambique is forty-seven. Mankell writes of a "strange European revolution in the mid-1950s that removed old age from our life experience and deleted death from our agenda. . . . Instead youth, energy, health are the dominant theme. Death has been transferred to the seniors' quarters. . . . When death disappeared we became poorer. European culture has been ravaged by the forces of the free market just as a forest is ravaged by clear-cutting."[12]

I would like to offer an example of this devastation, a story about the director of a large company. He hears that his son has been killed in an accident and he must identify the body. He refuses the tranquilizer offered to him by a kind policeman. His assistant suggests that he take the rest of the week off and offers to make the funeral arrangements for him. The manager declines, saying, "Thank you for the offer, but I'll manage. Please let the others know what happened. I would appreciate it if you would carry on as usual. No sympathy! Not a word about it!"

I do not know this person, but hearing this story makes me shudder. I can scarcely imagine how such a man could stand himself in his misfortune. He shows no weakness and allows no one else to show any. He will fail at his defeats, particularly at the ultimate one: dying. He is condemned to strength and to winning. If he ever gave a thought to his own death, I guess he would want to die in harness: a sudden heart attack at work, utterly painless.

I see this man as a good representative of the First World, who has learned something that cannot be taken for granted in other cultures and was unthinkable in our culture, too, just a few generations ago. He asserts himself; he gains a world for himself through action, by doing, giving shape to things. He . . . but it is unfair to say all this only in relation to him; I mean all of us, so let me say it: we. For a long time now we have done much more than merely tolerate our life experience. We no longer need to bow down in dumb deference to all that comes our way. We have become doers and have learned to see through the laws that govern processes; to intervene, banish illness, extend life, and to be makers of our own lives and our fate.

In this process the human capacity for pathos, our ability to experience suffering, atrophies. Accepting life, admitting our limits, considering life meaningful even in its fragmentariness and brokenness, are skills we are no longer learning. The person who has learned to live only in the action mode, who finds self-justification only by doing, cannot cope with situations in which there is nothing he or she can do anymore, when limits impose themselves on us as doers. Can a doer stand to be powerless sometimes? Can doers preserve their humanity even in life's defeats, if the meaning of their very being is defined exclusively by activity and the reproduction of life? Can they be sick or die? Or are sickness and death now only to be considered sites of dramatic absurdity, best never thought of at all, to be over-looked or denied?

"I would appreciate it if you would carry on as usual. No sympathy! Not a word about it!" says the manager. Business as usual. Go right on as if no one had fallen out of life and as if you didn't notice the huge crack in its foundations. But his son is dead—and things cannot go well if everyone acts as if nothing had happened, as if the world in which he lived still existed. Perhaps the father will become ill over his denial of death; perhaps, and this would be worse, he will become callous, hard, unable to feel pain and will keep on functioning at work without any sign of injury. But he has lost a part of his soul. His ability to grieve, to feel longing, to remember, is broken; he is unable to feel unhappy in his misfortune.

Death has no place in the landscape of life for those who are pure doers and winners. Our cemeteries are located outside the urban centers. We live in a landscape where everyone is young and strong, rich, intelligent, and good-looking—or must appear so. The weak, the old, the dying do not count. Thus life in its waning stages has no name. It is diffi-cult to die in this landscape of winners who manage without memory.

November Days

Perhaps a first step would be to overcome the unmitigated preservation of power over life when we remember the dead. But how is that possible when most people have no access to the cemetery? Are there other places and rituals that can sustain our ability to remember? I am always amazed when old people know the dates of their parents' deaths forty or fifty years later. As if the sound of the funeral masses, memorial services, or *Jorzeiten* still rang in their ears; as if life did not go so quickly and seamlessly; as if death were allowed in, even in the age of machines. And as if we could approach death without saying, "No sympathy! Not a word about it!"

A festival crosses several borders[13]

In the night when somoza was overthrown
and he had to leave the country
there was a festival in neighboring costa rica
the streets and parks full of cheering people

Only in the hospital the nurses and doctors
had to be there because four people died
they looked out the window to the park
finally one of them called his friends
and asked them to bring the dead out
to join the festival in the park

So the dead did not keep the living
away from the joy of the festival

nor did the living
leave the dead in the lurch
they were there
when nicaragua became free
the dead and the living

These days in November that are still designated as holidays in our calendars are important to me: Day of Mourning, Day of Prayer and Repentance, the Sunday of the Dead (*Trauertag, Buß- und Bettag, Totensonntag*). They make me remember. They send me to the cemetery, at least inwardly. They make me aware that I am not the giver of my own life. Into the cloak of my life is woven all the affection and tenderness of the people who are no longer here and whom I remember. I do not need to reinvent life or be the first to do everything. I also do not need to finish everything I would like to have done with my life. I can live life as a fragment, just as the lives of my dead loved ones were fragmentary. They teach me something I do not want to forget; they tell me that I am going to die. Every person who is close to me and who dies before me removes a peg from my own life's tent. The person who dies before me separates friends from friend. My parents, brothers, and sisters who have died say to me: What I have done you will also have to do—die. I found the following epitaph on an old gravestone: *Eram, quod es*: I was what you are (alive). *Eris, quod sum*: You will be what I am (dead).

The dead tell me something else: What I was able to do, you will also be able to do—die. It is hard work to leave life behind, but it is not impossible. The dead diminish my fear. And sometimes I think the dead give us warmth. Perhaps the coldness in our country is increasing precisely because the dead have no place anymore and we ban them from memory out of fear of our own dying. Part of being human is remembering; equally important is looking ahead to those who will come after us. In fact, one can define human beings as those who know the names of their grandparents and who take care of their grandchildren. There is an unscrupulous obsession with today, with now-ness, that is connected with forgetting the dead and that creates merciless consequences for all who are yet to be born. To be without memory is to have no need of a future.

One learns how to die by conceding that the dead person whose epitaph reads "You will be what I am" is right. This lesson should not be brought to one's attention at the end of life, but in the midst of living. All the religions of the world have known and practiced this awareness that we are finite and mortal. Remember—do not forget! That is one of the great commands in both Judaism and Islam. To forget God is to deny the reality of death, of what is small, old, and weak.

We are no longer needed—that is the real difficulty with growing old. But this not-being-needed does not need to turn into bitterness or despair. It can also lead to a kind of freedom in which I become freer, in which I have less fear and a greater sense of humor. I do not have to carry the weight of the world on my shoulders. It will not come to an end when I do. I am learning to let go of power and influence. If death really is more than an avoidable breakdown, if it is our sister, as Francis of Assisi thought, born with us and accompanying us like our shadow, then accepting it creates a kind of nonviolence in our dealings with others and with creation. It is not we who guarantee our life, this wonderful, self-renewing, indomitable life that is lent to us. This is not merely a philosophical insight; it is part and parcel of the belief in another guarantor of life.

I want to relate another example of such a manner of living with death. I am in the stage of life when I am aging and sometimes hear the master knocking. In 1994 I became seriously ill. After that my relationship to my adult children changed. I noticed they smiled about me more often than before, but not in a mean or impatient way. Somewhat amazed, really. They needed me less than before; I had already grown accustomed to that. The change that I cheerfully noted is a slow process of becoming smaller. Slowly the children took over the upbringing of their hard-to-teach mother. It was as if the old people, whom I had now joined, had become the children of the young.

A different relationship with death[14]

And when i asked you how you live
you began telling me about death

In a police van in bogota
on a street way up above the city
you figured
they would kill you

Already given up for dead
in intensive care
you started to put up a fight
there you called death stupid

Alongside the ordinary folks in nicaragua
you saw how differently they deal
with their many dead every day

The revolution is
a different relationship with death

Today twelve days afterward I notice
that you were telling me something about
    resurrection
when you talked about death

In my country people go to any amount of
    trouble
to overlook death
and no matter how high the cost
to avoid it

Today I know a little more about you
who when asked how he lives
begins to tell about death

A little more about a country
where people think dying
isn't the worst thing that can happen

And a little more
about resurrection
not enough yet

The Denial of Limits

The role that *terror mortis*, the fear of death, played in the old world has fundamentally changed. The old fears and the old consciousness of threats to life are no longer in the foreground, but largely forgotten and denied. In Martin Luther's world, which has a few things in common with the misery that has arisen in the world of the twentieth century, life expectancy was about a quarter of what we experience in the affluent world.

The new and totally different fears grow before our eyes along with the "third" technological revolution in which we find ourselves. Visionaries already offer us at least 130 or 150 years' life expectancy. Biotechnology, nanotechnology, and robotics promise to conquer old age, decrepitude, and death and at the same time to reprogram what to date have been known as Homo sapiens. It is no coincidence that Nazi terminology that had long since disappeared from discussions like these is reappearing: selection, eugenics, euthanasia. The ingenious scientific advances at the same time create new fears that I was able to detect already when my mother died. Are these advances not meant to make us into replaceable biomechanical beings that can be repaired and reproduced like any product one can come up with?

In the early '90s I was invited to speak on the theme of "limits" at a conference of the Technical University of Zurich. There was an impressive array of scholars from the natural sciences and philosophy. There was much talk of limited access, limitation, and eliminating limits (*Ausgrenzen, Begrenzen, Entgrenzen*), but the theme "death" was never mentioned; at least it did not appear anywhere in the program. I found it striking to talk about limits and no longer to mention the most natural limit of all. In this context I asked myself why our relationship to death is so immature. The theme of "eliminating limits" (*Entgrenzung*) is becoming more and more important for our understanding of reality. We live in a culture that wants to cross more and more boundaries. Every limit one sets oneself is regarded as old-fashioned and unnecessary. Whatever is faster, more, more frequent, and farther-reaching is unquestionably considered good and useful. This attitude of reaching beyond limits is being practiced in the most diverse forms. Persons who know exert power over objects and in the process lose their capacity to form relationships.

Before our eyes the rhythm of life is being deprived of limits. Whether it is summer or winter, we run around in thin shirts; the heat is always on, often excessive. Day and night play less and less of a role in our lives. The boundaries of space are being breached and thus abolished; distance and proximity are seen as more and more irrelevant. Time boundaries, too, are being abolished. Everyday life and holidays look more and more alike. In New York I saw a billboard that read, "We are open for you—24 hours a day, 7 days a week." Why not just say "always"? But then it would not be so pathetically obvious that we are also masters over time. Budgeting one's time, limitation, even the superfluous Jewish invention of the Sabbath, which suggests observing a day of rest once a week, must disappear, must be *entgrenzt*; the limitation of activity must be abolished. Limits are removable barriers or hindrances.

The feeling one gets with the total removal of life's limits appears at first glance as one of greater freedom and self-determination. We have learned to be doers, not merely passively experiencing life anymore. We have learned to see through the laws that govern processes, to overcome distances, to exert influence, to banish illnesses, and to extend life. We have become makers of our own lives, to a degree that was still unthinkable several generations ago. The denial of limits is desirable in the consumer culture, if not even declared essential.

Surely the abolition of limits that has occurred since the 1990s is far more radical than those I observed earlier. In the virtual world limits of space and time are no longer relevant. Genetic technology is fascinating because it abolishes limits of so-called natural life like nothing has ever done before and promises to step beyond them. I am referring here to a book by the title *Lizenz zum Töten* (*License to Kill*)[15] that reflects on the price of technical advances in medicine. The author mentions the limits of knowledge, but above all the limits of action. "It is possible to intervene in the genome, to repair defects or to prevent them. . . . It is possible to overcome limits of species. Whoever masters gene transfer can genetically modify plants, animals, and humans. It is possible to produce living trans-genetic beings."

Generational boundaries can now be suspended through deep-freezing and cloning. Different generations can be produced simultaneously. Aborted fetuses can be used as organ donors. It goes without saying that such possibilities awaken the old dreams of immortality. But the fact that all natural limits, such as menopause—these days certainly not a barrier to having children—can be eliminated creates new fears for me. All organs are becoming replaceable, which then also always means marketable.

In 1992 in Brazil I was with a family whose twelve-year-old child had not come home and they became worried. Suddenly someone said, "A little while ago some gringos [whites] went by—they need kidneys, don't they?" After a while the daughter got home, but the shock shook me deeply, right to the kidneys. But such fears have long since become the future reality in the world of abject poverty. Perhaps it is the total marketability of life that creates greater fear in me today than dying.

If it is true that equality, *égalité*, is an invention of death, then we should think of it as part of the exodus into a strange land, which is one of the foundations of Jewish piety. Abraham, whom Paul calls the "ancestor" (Rom 4:11)—unlike Odysseus—does not come to his senses and return home; instead he departs on a journey. Exodus is a basic motif of biblical religion. Arguably, one can think of Odysseus as the "archetype of modern subjectivity, which strives to assert itself and dominate."[16] From there the suppression of death follows as a matter of course.

Abraham does not return to the land of his forebears. He exposes himself to a foreign land—and that always means to the "Other." Part of the consciousness of death must be a degree of homelessness or not-yet-having-arrived. This is precisely what the new denial of death attempts to abolish, or at least to suppress. It is not only the equality of human beings that disappears in the world of affluence, but at the same time we lose that degree of not-being-at-home-anywhere that we all need to become human.

But can one ever really abolish this sense of homelessness? Would it even be desirable to get rid of what Heinrich Böll called this "because-we-aren't-quite-at-home-here"?

chapter two

Is Death the Last Enemy? The Theological Debate

Reunion with the Dead—a Blank Check: A Discussion with C. S. Lewis

I open this chapter with a book by the Anglican writer Clive S. Lewis (1898–1963), written after his wife had died of cancer. He had come to know this American writer, Joy Davidman, quite late in his life. She was a divorced Jewish woman and at one time a leading Communist journalist. She herself had become a Christian as a result of reading his books. When they were married in 1956, she was already ill with cancer and died four years later. In 1961 Lewis published *A Grief Observed*, pseudonymously at first; following his death it appeared under his name.[1]

The short book begins with this sentence: "No one ever told me that grief felt so like fear."[2] *Terror mortis* runs throughout the self-observation of this intellectual who did not abandon his critical mind after his conversion, who indeed was utterly unable to set it aside. "Talk to me about the truth of religion. . . . But don't come talking to me about the consolations of religion or I shall suspect that you don't understand. Unless, of course, you can literally believe all that stuff about family reunions 'on the further shore,' pictured in entirely earthly terms. But that is all unscriptural, all out of bad hymns and lithographs. There is not a word of it in the Bible."[3] A mother who has lost her child will not see him again. "The specifically maternal happiness must be written off. Never, in any place or time, will she have her son on her knees, or bathe him, or tell him a story, or plan for his future, or see her grandchild."[4] These are harsh, bitter sentences with which Lewis dismisses so unambiguously the pious lies about meeting again. Lewis interprets Paul's words—do "not grieve as others do who have no hope" (1 Thess 4:13)—ironically as being "so obviously addressed to our betters," not to us. Not to him. They "can comfort only those who love God better than the dead, and the dead better than themselves."[5]

Hard words like those are based on Lewis's clear understanding that God can never be used as a means to an end. The naïve child's prayer, *"Lieber Gott, mach mich fromm, dass ich in den Himmel komm"* (Dear God, give me piety so that I may go to heaven), does not manifest love of God but the utility, the "handiness" of God. Every mystic knew that love always excludes all purposes whatsoever.

Love is what it is, *sunder warumbe*—without a why or wherefore, as Meister Eckhart puts it in his wonderful phrase.[6] In Lewis's philosophical mind, the meaning of that phrase is this: "If you are approaching Him not as the goal but as a road, not as the end but as a means, you're not really approaching Him at all. That's what was really wrong with all those popular pictures of happy reunions 'on the further shore'; not the simple-minded and very earthly images, but the fact that they make an End of what we can get only as a by-product of the true End."[7] I am not clear about whether it would be better to give up on that "by-product" from the outset, that is, whether the "immortality of the soul," this basic concept of Greek philosophy, should not be removed altogether from its infelicitous fusion with the resurrection of the dead in Christian theology. I think it is possible to love the dead better than ourselves, but I would like to talk the author out of the preceding formulation: to "love God better than the dead."

This book by Lewis wrestles with these questions, and it is noteworthy because of the utter honesty of the author, who simply cannot see himself submitting to what Henning Luther called "the lies of the comforters." "The fruition of God. Reunion with the dead. These can't figure in my thinking except as counters. Blank cheques. . . . The reality of either—the cashing of either cheque—would probably blow all one's ideas about both (how much more one's ideas about their relation to each other) into smithereens. The mystical union on the one hand. The resurrection of the body, on the other. I can't reach the ghost of an image, a formula, or even a feeling, that combines them," writes Lewis.[8]

This contrast does indeed sum up the problem of a "mysticism of death" in a sharp and clear manner. One of my fundamental questions is whether eternal life can be thought of together with the immortality of the individual—indeed, whether one must be able to think of the former together with the latter. I have doubts about the second blank check, the reunion with the dead.

At the end, Lewis is once again completely pious. He quotes the words of his dying wife, spoken not to him but to the chaplain. "'I am at peace with God.' She smiled, but not at me. *Poi si tornò all' eterna fontana.*"[9] With this return to the eternal spring, in Dante's formulation, the book draws to its end.

The First Death Is the Death of the Other, or Critique of Ego-Thanatology

When my father was dying, I read poems by Goethe to him. "Human soul, how you are like the water; human fate, how you are like the wind." My mother was busy denying reality, clinging to the idea that "It'll be okay again." When I—helplessly—said to Father, "But you are not alone," he replied, "Where I go, everyone goes alone. Everyone." I had my helpless doubts about that but did not dare even to stammer, "No, Papa, no." Even though that is what I felt.

The idea that death is always the death of an individual who is then left to her- or himself is widely held. Irrespective of whoever influences our life for good or for ill, according to this idea the individual her- or himself must bring it to an end, independent of sympathy or support. Death is not transferable. However reasonable and persuasive that may sound, there are now new questions about this "ego-thanatological blindness" that philosopher and author Michael Mayer examines in his book *Totenwache* (*Deathwatch*), written after his father's death in an accident.[10]

According to Mayer, it is inadequate to narrow the scope of the question to the death that everyone has to die her- or himself. He attempts a deconstruction of Western philosophy of death that has been related since Stoicism to the death of the individual. In the *memento mori*, individuals are to prepare themselves for their own dying. His book is a philosophical experiment, often somewhat fanciful stylistically and brittle, but important in that it seeks to lead us out of a prison. That prison can be described as the nontransferability of death, the absolute sense that death is always my own. Death is always death of an individual who is finally left to her- or himself. Only the individual can experience this death, and the meaning of death can be discerned exclusively from the perspective of the first-person singular.

The philosopher Wilhelm Schmid even associates this traditional view, one that my father shared, with a kind of pride, not only with despair. In a radio broadcast he said that in the face of nontransferable death, the individual can insist, "This is my death, I make it my own, hold on to it as my possession, and won't let it be taken from me by others who seek to determine how it will happen."[11]

But is death "my possession"? Does death belong to the ego? Does it threaten me above all? Michael Mayer discusses the death of the other; the title *Deathwatch*, alluding to an antiquated custom of piety, makes that point quite clearly. The engagement with death takes place at the "watch" or "wake" for someone who has died. This could be a place for reflection and learning.

Mayer draws especially on the work of Jewish philosopher Emmanuel Levinas (1906–1995), who reflects on the death of someone else as "the first death." "[It] is not my nonbeing that causes anxiety, but that of the loved one or of the other, more beloved than my being. What we call, by a somewhat corrupted term, love, is *par excellence* the fact that the death of the other affects me more than my own. The love of the other is the emotion of the other's death. It is my receiving the other—and not the anxiety of death awaiting me—that is the reference to death."[12] In this different way of thinking, the reflecting I, the *cogito ergo sum*—I think, therefore I am—is disempowered. According to Levinas, this *I* must be depicted in the accusative; that is, it exists as something that is addressed, needed, appealed to.[13] In Levinas's philosophical language, which lets his rootedness in Jewish religion shine through but rarely names it. The human being is used by the other; indeed, one person is "the hostage of the other," lives in "the condition of one taken hostage,"[14] in responsibility for the other that cannot be relativized. That is why it is not my—potential—death that threatens me most, but that of the other.

Levinas has helped me better to understand the increasingly absolute individualism under which we live.[15] *Homo incurvatus in se* was how Martin Luther defined the sinner. It is a challenge to Judeo-Christian religion that this "human being turned in on the self" has become a central aim of our economy. This calls for resistance. In Levinas, the *I* belongs in the accusative before any nominative form.[16] The *I* is not, as Descartes put it, "the master and owner of nature." Religion's chief end is not the freedom of the individual, but the ability to relate, which Martin Buber expresses in sentences such as "He, she is like you," or "In the beginning was relation." The concept of the neighbor is, on the inter-religious scale, the greatest gift of the Jewish people to humankind. Remembering God is possible only when the *I* is in the accusative: it is placed under judgment as well as needed.

A Christian theologian, Henning Luther (1947–1991), facing his own death of HIV/AIDS, learned from Levinas above all "passionately not to desire [the death of the other human being]. . . . My death that I ponder is always merely a fictive death, a death anticipated intellectually. . . . Eschatological hope as a protest against the death of others is, therefore, not oriented toward my own immortality."[17]

Elsewhere Henning Luther sharply criticizes "the lies of the comforters" that arise with the individualization of death and with the style of pastoral care that has so utterly aligned itself with it. "Christian faith does not in the first instance offer comfort, certitude, and reassurance. Rather, it interrupts the normality of our life, calls us out, lets us set out (Abraham), and search for home."[18] The Epistle to the Hebrews 13:14, says that "Here we have no lasting city, but we are looking for the city that is to come." In this view, faith leads into a homelessness that suffers from the world we live in. The homelessness increases with the barbarity of our world.

I heard a good joke about death. A very old farmer up in the high mountains receives a visit from his pastor, who affably asks, "So how are we doing?" The limping farmer replies, "Ah, you know, Reverend, the main thing is that our Lord God stays healthy!" Perhaps a mysticism of death could be formulated that way.

Paul as a Mystic of Death, or "Who Will Rescue Me from This Body of Death?" (Rom 7:24)

I cannot believe that "Death is the wages of sin" (Rom 6:23); it cannot mean that every starving child is to blame for his own death! Even less can I believe that death is supposed to be "the last enemy" (1 Cor 15:26). Is death in truth Friend Hein (*Freund Hein*— an old German expression for death) or "sleep's brother" or even the longed-for "sweet death" that

Bach intones? The unknown poet who wrote that phrase, which became known in 1724, begs death, "Come, lead me into peace, for I am tired of this world."

The Christian understanding of death has many different voices. Paul thinks not primarily of the physical death of the individual but of the all-pervasive, anti-godly power of destruction that rules this world. It is the empire that peddles itself as *pax romana* while spreading slavery all over the world. Paul understands the world of his time as one in which human beings are held captive with no chance of escape because they are under the totalitarian rule of sin. In his Epistle to the Romans, the word "sin" occurs forty-eight times in the singular. By contrast, the actual sinful deeds of human beings that we think of chiefly in connection with "sin" or "sinning" occur there only seven times. Paul thinks of sin not in an individualistic sense but as a social reality that governs and shapes human beings in the Roman Empire. The central assertions about sin "all have a common denominator: they are conceived of in terms of relations of domination (and not in categories of guilt and of action)."[19]

Paul's reality is not that of Rome's magnificent buildings, baths, and banquets. On his missionary journeys he always set out from the Jewish congregations he was visiting. He knew their reality: heavy physical labor and bitter poverty as well as the ever-recurring coercion to show veneration for the imperial ruler, a practice that often violated the Torah of the Jewish people. Emperor Caligula (37–41 C.E.) decreed that his statue be erected in the Temple of Jerusalem and that, accordingly, he be recognized as a divinity. It is interesting to note that it was only fairly late that Roman emperors had themselves addressed as *Dominus*, something emperors Augustus and Tiberius had still drastically prohibited because that would designate their subjects as slaves.[20]

Roman historian Tacitus calls a spade a spade in naming the suffering of the majority of people under Roman rule: they are slaves.[21] That is precisely what Paul also knew. He calls this dominion of slavery "sin," and death is the consequence of submission to sin. Which death is meant here?

It is not the demise, the finitude of humans, dying as in our normal understanding of death. It is something altogether different: the submission to the tyrannical rule of sin. Paul saw sin ruling, an omnipotent God-denying power of destruction that demanded worship in the Roman world. He speaks of "the sting of death" (1 Cor 15:56); the Greek word *kentron*—sting—refers to a rod fitted with iron spikes, used for driving animals and torturing slaves. The words "death" and "sin" are nearly interchangeable for Paul; both have their "role as world-dominators and slave-drivers."[22] The human being is "sold under sin" (Rom 7:14). Paul ends his desperate lament in Romans 7 with a personal cry: "Wretched man that I am! Who will rescue me from this body of death?" (vv. 17-18, 24).

Neurologist Rudolf Kautzky has translated some of Paul's texts differently and in more everyday language, including the one just mentioned. "Strictly speaking, it is not I who act but the egotism that rules over me. I know that this is not as it ought to be, but I cannot cope with myself and so I act against my better judgment. Miserable man that I am! Who sets me free from this burden that prevents life from being what it is meant to be?"[23]

Paul uses different words to name the world-domination of sin: it exercises royal rule; it is a *kyrios*, but not in the subsequent liturgical sense of Christians. Rather, sin rules as a lord and slave owner who issues laws and wages war. "Its world-wide instrument of domination is death"; its law of sin is "the very coercion that makes it impossible to fulfill God's will, the Torah."[24]

Albert Schweitzer (1875–1965) interpreted Paul's doctrine of redemption as mysticism. He sees the necessity of dying not in the sense of physical demise but, in an entirely this-worldly way, as an ethic of redemption in which humans are no longer coerced to serve idols. According to Schweitzer, Paul does not regard Christianity as a new religion but as a continuation of Judaism. In this sense Paul was not the "hellenizer of Christianity." To die and to rise with Christ means for Schweitzer to enter into the other way of being, namely that of God's reign. Here mysticism does not necessarily mean "being one with God," but more "being in Christ as having died and risen with him." It is engaging to see how "the mysticism of the Apostle Paul" in Schweitzer's thought corresponds to the starting point of current feminist-liberation theology and its ethics, precisely in the respect that it relates not merely to the individual.[25]

In his reflections on a philosophy of culture, Schweitzer had suggested that all profound philosophy, all profound religion, was finally nothing other than a struggle for ethical mysticism and mystical ethics. His concepts of mysticism and ethics constantly flow one into the other here. It was there that he drew on his interpretation of Paul, saying that an ethic that satisfies the mind has to be born in mysticism, indeed, that it must desire to be rooted in the mysticism of relatedness with everything that lives. He uses an image to sum up his point: "Mysticism . . . is not the flower but only the chalice of the flower. The flower is ethics." This is the most beautiful rendition of my somewhat dry summary sentence: "Mysticism is resistance." For him mysticism is "only a different term for the eschatological notion of redemption."[26] Here the eternal and the ethical are thought of as a unity, just as the ancient mystics sought to think of the good, the beautiful, and the true as a unity.

Today we too live in a world that is comparable to the Roman Empire, where cooperating with and submitting to the idols that rule over us are to be understood in Paul's sense as "being-in-death." Our idols have different names that may be called "cash" and "fun"; our being-in-death looks quite sophisticated and enduring. What today may be called "*pax americana*"—I learned this expression from friends in the American peace movement—is a system arranged for the self-enrichment of 20 percent of humankind and that puts up with the impoverishment of the rest and with the destruction of creation. New forms of slavery, such as the treatment of slave women in the textile industry that produces our wonderfully cheap T-shirts, or the increasing number of sex-slave women worldwide, deliver a clear language. The description of the *pax romana* fits perfectly the neoliberalism under which we live. When will we learn with and from Paul to long for deliverance "from this body of death"?

The "body of death" that we all live in signifies the very impediment to genuine living that is oriented toward relatedness with the neighbor. Buber says of the neighbor that "he, she is like you." In our world, death is the destruction of every kind of mutuality. The individual's "enlightened self-interest" has become the sole rule in an increasingly "deregulated" world.

For Paul, the slavery of sin that he calls "death" came to an end in Christ. Resurrection acted out means rising up against the kind of death that permits life merely to keep on vegetating. Our taking part in resurrection from slavery is essential. Kautzky gives a new translation of the sentence of 1 Cor 15:17 that Martin Luther had rendered this way: "But if Christ has not been raised, your faith is futile and you are still in your sins." With his eye clearly on present conditions in the church, Kautzky brings this reading into sharp focus: "We claim that Jesus was raised from the dead, but we do not allow this claim to come true. Thus, we still keep on vegetating instead of living."[27]

"A different world is possible." This is a wonderful statement of today's opponents of globalization. They could also exclaim with Paul, "This we know:

we have let go of our old order of values and are no longer dependent on 'having'" (Kautzky's rendition of Rom 6:6). There is resurrection from the death that enslaves us. We have become free.

The Gospel of Philip, found in the literature of early Christianity, expresses the same knowledge of what "death" and "life" mean in the following sentence, which sounds crazy but is thought-provoking: "A pagan does not die; he has never lived and so cannot die."[28] Is that Christian arrogance? We have to understand this in the context of what Paul has to say about death within Roman slavery. Slavery is no longer noticed; the subjugated do not see it, nor does it bother the slave owners.

The *pax americana* has far outstripped the *pax romana*, above all by means of its superior staging and the more astute marketing of itself. The *pax americana* is utterly taken for granted by now. And as far as impoverishment goes, that only affects others, anyway. The fourth logion of *The Gospel of Philip* continues, "Whoever has believed in the truth, has lived, and is in danger of dying."[29] Are we of that company?

Erich Fromm: A Jewish Teacher

To be able to think of finitude and eternal life together is a goal toward which I have been slowly feeling my way. I would like to add another chapter to my lifework, one I had put aside at the time I was writing *The Silent Cry: Mysticism and Resistance.* I would like to describe death as a "place" or locus of mystical experience, as I had done before for nature, eroticism, suffering, community, and joy.

Theology of liberation was a decisively new phenomenon in the 1970s. It calls for a clear orientation toward this world. The God who listens to the cry of his people in Egypt sets us free—here and now and not in some other world. That theology renders the Greek word *soteria*, which actually means "rescue," for example from shipwreck or slavery, as "liberation" in place of redemption. This different perception became for me a theological release from superfluous ballast. Liberation for life is so much more than redemption from life. The dreadful German children's prayer "Dear God, give me piety, so that I may go to heaven," was unbearable for me for two reasons. For one, it expresses a *do ut des* (I give so that you might give) that corresponds to an ideal of capitalism: when I give you something, you in turn must give me something. For another, I did not want to go to heaven later but, with Heinrich Heine, "already here on earth."

The chief difficulty I had with traditional theology was the problem of my generation with "the Lord who so wondrously reigneth," as the hymn "Praise Ye the Lord, the Almighty, the King of Creation" puts it. I had made it plain already at the German *Kirchentag* of 1965 that I could not praise a lord conceived that way. How could one still talk that way after all that had taken place? "Ponder anew what the Almighty can do, who with His love doth befriend thee"—and where was he in Auschwitz? This question led me to a "theology after the death of God," to "believing in God atheistically." Those were titles of my first books, contradictory assertions or dialectical formulations that only later became clarified with the help of an emerging feminist and liberation theology.

Erich Fromm (1900–1980) critiqued authoritarian religion and its aims of obedience and submissiveness; it helped me a lot. His references to a humanistic-utopian understanding of the biblical tradition, especially of the prophets, lifted me out of the prison of false obedience.

The religious experience of oneness with the totality of Being, which includes greater joy and greater vulnerability, is, however, constitutive only for one type of religion, the "humanitarian" as opposed to the "authoritarian" type. Erich Fromm's distinction is at odds with the customary distinctions between religions, such as theistic versus nontheistic. Authoritarian religion is the acknowledgment of a higher, invisible power that has the right to demand obedience, adoration, and worship. God is powerful authority, while human beings are powerless and of no significance. Humans are to denigrate their value and strength. The essential element of authoritative religion is submissiveness to a power beyond humans, and, hence, in this view, the chief virtue is obedience.

One of my favorite sentences from Fromm's *Psychoanalysis and Religion*[30] says that the real conflict is not between faith in God and atheism, but between a humanistic religious disposition and a stance that amounts to idol worship, irrespective of how that is consciously expressed or disguised.

I'd like to tell a story about this. Between September 1943 and July 1944, there was a family camp in Auschwitz where the children lived who had been transported there from Terezin and who wrote postcards, intended by the authorities to deceive international public opinion. In that camp—and now comes a story of resurrection—various forms of education were pursued. The children who had already been selected to be gassed were taught French, mathematics, and music. The educators did their work fully aware of the hopelessness of the situation. Denuded of value themselves, they taught their pupils how to know the world. Destroyed themselves, they taught the opposite: nondestruction, life. Stripped of dignity themselves, they restored the dignity of the human being. Someone may say, "It didn't do them any good." But that is how pagans talk. Let us say instead: it does make a difference. Let us say in an utterly this-worldly way: God makes a difference.

In a conversation on religion, Erich Fromm made reference to the One. "It is a principle that has no name; no image can be made of it, whereas idols are things that humans construct themselves. Idols are the work of human hands, to which they submit themselves." Fromm distinguishes between divinity and the "god who has created, who rewards and punishes," the deity that had become problematic for him. While the radical humanists, of whom he is a representative example, can still "understand those theistic manifestations of the idea of the ONE poetically, they can no longer regard them as their language."[31]

What I would ask Fromm here is this: What language do radical humanists speak then? Or do they simply fall silent when, even though they can understand such language poetically, they don't speak it? Does there not have to be another language of humanism? Does the scientific mode of expression suffice? Is that language, forbidding and superseding all other language, not also a sort of idolatry? Since the beginning of the new century, which I like to date from the year 1989, that is, with the *Wende*, the fall of Communism and the resulting rise of the autocratic rule of capitalism, an old sentence of Martin Luther has been on my mind: "Reason is a whore"; that is, it sleeps with everyone who pays. One look at gene technology is enough to confirm Luther's point.

Surely one of the reasons Fromm has been forgotten in so many places today is that humanist speech has fallen silent. As I see it, the totalitarian rule of the technocratic language of science is one of the fundamental problems that points us back to the old human languages of *religio*. What does it mean, I ask Erich Fromm, to say, "to understand something poetically," when we have given up speaking those old languages? I agree with him that the alternative to God is the veneration of idols—a basic thought of Judaism. The Protestant Reformer Luther repeats this when he says that human beings are always a riding animal—either the Devil or Christ rides them— a thought that neatly subverts the illusion that is widely held today in post-religious being and thinking. I am critical of the fear of *religio* and what it connects with. I think that is wrong. But I also think at times that Erich Fromm was perhaps more Jewish than he wanted to admit.

Becoming More and More Jewish

I have become more and more Jewish in the past fifteen years. For me that does not mean retrogression into the authoritative forms of religion. What it does suggest is that I acknowledge various reappraisals of a "theology after Auschwitz." An error of fundamentalism is the belief that because God allowed Auschwitz to happen, God must also have wanted it to happen, since nothing on earth happens without God's will.[32] Jewish thinkers like Abraham Joshua Heschel have spoken of "God in need of men," that God needs human beings. God has to have friends or else God has no power. In Auschwitz God was anything but a powerful potentate; rather, God was small and weak because there were almost no friends in Germany to stand with God. The notion of God's power must be conceived in a new and different way than in the prevailing theology. Reciprocal help, reciprocal reliance, and mutual dependence are basic requirements even at the biological level of life on our planet. And so a theology of mutuality would have to provide, in addition to the deconstructive work of critique of patriarchy, a constructive program that includes a new ecofeminist understanding of creation that at the same time remains committed to Scripture and tradition.

In addition to Martin Buber, Erich Fromm, and Abraham Heschel—I name them in the order that I discovered them—I want to mention Emmanuel Levinas, who is one of those great teachers who helped me understand the "incurvation on the self" more clearly.

Becoming more and more Jewish also means for me to become more related to creation. I come from an educated, middle-class, almost post-Christian family. I found my way into religion through Christ, through what he did, how he lived and suffered, which was communicated to me by a woman who taught religion.[33] Today, I view my theological thinking of that time as being too "Christocentric," and, paying less attention to the second article of the Apostles' Creed, I have since concentrated more on the Spirit, the *ruach*, and on the first article, the belief in the Creator.

This turn to creation is related to something else that is deeply rooted in liberation theology. For a liberation theology, victims are always the point of departure for perception and other actions. We have to ask about the "losers" and not about the "winners." And so it is necessary to see poor Mother Earth, who is slowly being tortured to death, alongside the poor who are deprived of their rights. Do not the resistance movements we were able to observe in Seattle, Prague, Nice, Davos, and Porto Alegre (January 2001) also turn their attention to the economic and ecological catastrophes that globalization from above accepts into the deal that favors the winners?

With Matthew Fox, I see our Mother, the earth, hanging on the cross today. That has an inner perspective as well, which points to the destruction of every form of creatureliness. Some time ago I watched a talk show with a man who wants to have himself put on ice, injected with antifreeze, taken into a refrigerated building, and, after two or three hundred years, when this nuisance of death won't happen anymore, thawed again. The procedure and storage costs amount to only $37,000, he noted coolly. What was most dreadful for me was that this man did not appear to me any more afflicted or disturbed than we all are! Is the breakdown we call death not avoidable too, like so many things that people accepted centuries ago as fate? That's one of the basic issues with the megalomania that prevails in the present.

The eminent Swiss sociologist Jean Ziegler established as early as 1975, in his book *Die Lebenden und der Tod* (*The Living and Death*), how the consciousness of mortality and powerlessness is obstructed by the blinders in the dominant culture of today. He proposed the thesis that "the way to overcome the consumer society leads through the rediscovery of death."[34]

I want to embed this rediscovery of death in a different reflection. I suspect that our understanding of creation within the world of machines is somewhat damaged. God did not create the world as a potter makes a pot, as a designer builds a machine, as a completed thing that one throws away when it doesn't work anymore. Creation is determined by a rhythm, a change that we experience as day and night, summer and winter, ebb and flow, warmth and cold, youth and old age. When God, in the biblical narrative, looks upon everything at the end and finds it to be "very good," what is meant is not perfection, permanence, unchanging existence, but this rhythm of life.

I love it: the change of seasons is for me not a regrettable nuisance, something to be avoided, but—I almost want to use really very old-fashioned language—a part of "earthly" life that lives from, by, and within this change. What makes me afraid is the technocratic certainty that everything there is on earth is always at our disposal and can be bought: strawberries even in December, spring weather for tourists any time of the year, sex even in old age, and never-ending amusement—called "fun" in the *lingua franca* of today. The element of time, coming and going, the rhythm of life are canceled out in favor of immediate availability to our disposal. The more virtual the world gets, the less we need to perceive that the leaves on the trees come and go. Schoolchildren no longer know that an onion, planted in the earth, needs time to sprout a tiny green tip. They do know how many buttons to push in order to turn things on or off; what they know no longer is the rhythm of life that we ourselves did not establish, that was created by someone other than us.

When I get the feeling that God probably had something else in mind with creation, it becomes most apparent to me that we are still just standing by, allowing creation to be destroyed piece by piece before our eyes by the delusion of omnipotence and greed for possessions. When I repeat with others, "I believe in God, the Creator. . . ," it is not an explanation or even an analysis of the world; it is much rather a declaration of love that relates to this rhythm of life. We can feel it, we can suffer it. We can even sing praises to it.

We need a new spirituality that knows and accepts the rhythm of life. We can interrupt ourselves in order to perceive that rhythm and attune ourselves to it. It is there before we are and will be there after us. "The great does not remain great, nor small what is small, the night has twelve hours and then there comes day," as Bertolt Brecht puts it.[35] This kind of hope can survive only when we learn to consent to this rhythm.

The concept of ecofeminism is not quite at home yet among us, but I regard it as indispensable because it brings into sharp focus the need to take sides with the victims of technocratic globalization. The earth and, in the same way, the overwhelming majority of the poor, who are women, are treated by the powers that govern as a material resource, as usable objects. In this context, ecofeminism is the rebellion against and the radical critique of that understanding of science to which Descartes perhaps gave most precise expression when he spoke of human beings as "*maîtres et possesseurs de la nature*," masters and owners of nature. "Human beings" for him naturally meant the white European male whose relationship to slaves, women, and nature is all the same: he is lord, possessor, and user of all these objects.

In this sense, ecofeminism is a further development of liberation theology; it builds on the latter. But at the same time it—finally!—corrects some of

the great weaknesses in this theology that originated in Latin America. Ecofeminism corrects a
certain androcentrism inherent in it and its overly
self-assured thinking that takes too little notice of
the earth. Women were left unnoticed and unheard,
including even "Pachamama," as the Aymara people of Bolivia call the earth, the mother of life. An
anthropocentrism that relates exclusively to human
beings and their power to dispose has damaged
Christianity no less than the other destructive phe-
nomena fundamental to our culture, such as racism,
class dominance, and sexism. A liberating theology begins with the break with those traditions of
domination, exploitation, and submission. Reverting
to premodernity is not a cute romantic game but a
necessity. Today, in the interest of the survival of
all, we need a new relationship to the earth. Among
the most important forms that relationship takes is
to accept the finitude of life and to consent to its
natural rhythm. At the heart of a different, nonan-
thropocentric relation to life must be a multifaceted
reflection on death such as that contributed by Latin
American women. The spirituality that is sought in
this relationship is one of the fundamental changes
we need. Accepting the finitude of life and the transitoriness of the *I* relates us to all other living creatures. In the end it finally turns possessors and users
into brothers and sisters. That is how we can learn
to have more of a reason to sing, "Every part of this
earth is holy for my people." Even the cemetery.

chapter three

Women and Death

Jesus Died Differently from Socrates

I began to think about death when I was asked in 1961 to write a radio commentary on the Passion. Eventually it was given the title "Jesus Died Differently from Socrates." Taking a detour by way of another innocent man who goes to his death, although he could save himself, was helpful to me. The detour led me to Athens, to the beginning of the fourth century B.C.E. There, Socrates, son of Sophroniskos the sculptor and Phainarete the midwife, was sentenced to death for alleged impiety, just as Jesus was handed over to the authorities by Caiphas, the high priest, for blasphemy (Matt 26:65ff.). Both of these accused men were tried, found guilty, and sentenced to death.

Socrates drank his cup of poison in the year 399 B.C.E. In his *Phaedo* Plato described in exact detail how his teacher died. Well-meaning friends wanted to help Socrates escape from prison, but he rejected this offer of help because he did not want to violate the laws of the state in which he lived. A friend of Jesus, Peter, gives Jesus similar advice: "Lord, save yourself! This must never happen to you" (Matt 16:22).[1] But Jesus travels to Jerusalem, knowing what danger lurks for him there. Later, too, he rejects yet another offer of assistance by Peter, who this time wants to use his sword.

The manner in which these two innocents die, however, is utterly different. For one thing, there is the objective difference in the killing methods used. But just as important is the distinction to be made between the two figures in their thinking and behavior. The Athenian practice of poisoning criminals to death is infinitely more humane than the slow suffocation to death on a cross, often taking days, that was called for by the *pax romana* for its most heinous criminals and insurgents. Also different is the place of death. The Athenian prison has a bath that Socrates uses prior to dying. Family and friends are allowed to join him there. By contrast, crucifixions allowed no intimacy; they were a form of slow, public torture. Viewers who would taunt and boo loudly were politically desirable.

Perhaps the most astonishing element in Socrates's dying is his calm good humor, which is utterly absent in Jesus' case. The night of Jesus' arrest begins with his "quivering and quaking." He tells his friends that he is "deeply grieved, even to death" (Mark 14:34). Jesus dies not as a hero and not as a wise man, superior to others. Socrates comforts his weeping friends.

Jesus weeps and looks to his friends for comfort, but they have fallen asleep. He complains, "So, could you not stay awake with me one hour?" (Matt 26:40). He needs them but is abandoned. Jesus' plea "Stay with me and watch with me,"[2] remains unheard. It can still be heard today in liturgical forms, and it was only when I heard the song from Taizé that incorporates these words of Jesus that I realized that Jesus continues to plead with us to stay with him in the thousands of voices of those suffering today, the starving, the tortured.

Crito, a friend of Socrates, attempts to postpone the hour of death. Perhaps they can celebrate one last time over a shared meal; the sun has, after all, not yet set. Socrates waves him away. He is ready. *Phaedo* reports that after Socrates had bathed and his three sons, two young ones and an older one, had been brought to him, and the women belonging to his entourage had arrived, he spoke with them all in Crito's presence. *Phaedo* then concludes, "He gave certain directions as to his wishes; he then told the women and children to leave, and himself returned to us."[3] Socrates wants his experience of dying to take place in the context of his philosophical discussions with his friends and pupils.

The exclusion of women from rituals of dying is very unusual in the history of religion. In most cultures the care of and companionship to the dying, as well as the washing and anointing of the dying, are matters belonging to women, as are the rituals of weeping and lamenting the dead. Jesus is quite aware of this. While his disciples consider it absurdly wasteful when a woman anoints him in Bethany, Jesus sees it as a preparation for his death (Matt 26:12). The women seem to live closer to death than the dominant sex. But for Socrates, who with such confidence distinguishes between the transitory physical body and the immortality of the soul, this is irrelevant.

With gentle irony Socrates says to the slave who brings him the cup of poison, "I understand, but at least one may pray to the gods, and so one should, that the removal from this world to the other will be a salutary one! That is my own prayer: so may it be."[4] Then he put the cup to his lips and drank it without the least distaste, with a noble bearing, up to the end.

The "removal from this world to the other" assumes the immortality of the soul. In his defense before the court, Socrates makes the distinction between two possible interpretations of death—that of an eternal sleep without feeling or dreaming, and that of a crossing over. "But if death is a departure from this place to another, and it is true what people say that all who have died are there, then what bliss could be greater than this."[5] Socrates is inclined to this second interpretation, and one need not fear the crossing over into a better life.

Did Jesus not know this? Why would he not let himself be comforted with the immortality of the soul? The true philosopher, the friend and lover of wisdom, lives without fear of death. Socrates asks, "Would it not be irrationality itself if such a person feared death?" To this way of thinking, death appears as the liberator from the prison of the body. Idealism's belief in the next world devalues this life as a school for the next, this world as a laboratory for the next, so that human beings need no comfort in dying.

Socrates lived in a world that was distant from his self, focused on being as close as possible to death. He was able to overcome dying. He died free of fear and at peace; he remained completely in control, which is exactly what one cannot say about Jesus. Jesus did not face death as a sovereign being, free of fear; on the contrary, he suffered in dying. The immortality of the soul that carried Socrates was not Jesus' thing. Jesus lived in an intimacy that was focused on this life, not on another. He lived in an intimacy with death that, because it knew fear, was also full of hope, not for another life but for the Other who loves this, our life.

The insight that the first death we know is always the death of another is not a twentieth-century discovery. Plato's wonderfully exact description in *Phaedo* demonstrates this.

> Till then most of us had been fairly well able to restrain our tears; but when we saw he was drinking, that he'd actually drunk it, we could do so no longer. In my own case, the tears came pouring out in spite of myself, so that I covered my face and wept for myself—not for Socrates, no, but for my own misfortune in being deprived of such a man for a companion. . . . Apollodoros, who even earlier had been continuously in tears, now burst forth

into such a storm of weeping and grieving, that he made everyone present break down except Socrates himself. But Socrates said: "What a way to behave, my strange friends! Why, it was mainly for this reason that I sent the women away, so that they shouldn't make this sort of trouble; in fact, I've heard one should die in silence. Come now, calm yourselves and have strength." When we heard this, we were ashamed and checked our tears.[6]

Jesus died differently. The men had abandoned him. According to the oldest accounts, they had fled (Matt 25:56 and Mark 16:8). Perhaps there were women present as he uttered his last cry, which was neither silent nor comforting, but a prayer of lament from the Psalms: *"Eli, Eli, lema sabachthani"* (Ps 22:1). Jesus collapses, crying out; a man deprived of all comfort accuses his God. For the church father Augustine, this cry—incidentally, the only word from the cross included by both of the oldest gospel writers in their narratives—is so unbearable that he refused to believe it was true. He thought that Jesus could not have spoken this way; it must have been the Adam in him, the first human being, speaking such words.

As the story continues to the Resurrection, it is the women—admissible as court witnesses only in exceptional cases according to Roman law—who assume the role of messengers. One can add: the role of angels.

Birth and Death

"Dying . . . apes birth. When we die we're as helpless and naked as newborn children. The death shroud is our diaper. What good does it do? Our whimpering does just about as much good in the grave as it does in the cradle."[7]

Death has often been described in terms of birth. Martin Luther compares death with birth in his "Sermon on Preparing to Die": "What happens here in dying is just like a child being born, full of danger and fears, out from its little dwelling place in its mother's body. . . . So, too, is the path we take in leaving this life through the narrow portal of death. . . . Thus the dying of the dear saints is called a new birth and their feast days are called *natale*, Latin for the day of their birth."[8] Traditionally death was often understood not as the opposite of life—as in modernity—but birth and death belonged together; they are polarities that condition one other. The newborn baby often looks like a wizened old woman. Arriving and "going home" have much to do with one another.

Is it only a coincidence that in the Romance languages "life" and "death," *vita* and *mors*, are feminine words? Here I want to bring in two examples from worlds that are foreign to me. One is from Greek antiquity. The goddess Hecate was goddess of the underworld; as a three-headed ruler, she terrified the living with torches and nooses, snakes and horrific barking of hounds. Originally she was also the goddess of fertility. She fostered the growth of the herds and saw to it that young people thrived. As the goddess of the moon, she was seen as the secret protectress in the night; she protected streets and gates. She was loved and admired by women above all. Perhaps this is why women's relationship with death is traditionally so different from what it became in the modern era, which is similar to Socrates's relationship to death. Hecate symbolized both processes—being born and having to die—which for centuries were considered "natural," unchangeable realities.

The other example is from the present, from Palestine. The writer Sumaya Farhat-Naser, in her book, whose Arabic title translates *Rooted in the Land of the Olive Trees*, offers a precise description of grief and of dealing with injured souls. "It is customary in our culture that in order to show one's last respects for one's dying bridegroom, there is not only weeping, but the bridegroom's mother is expected to cry out with joyous warbling. It seems grotesque, but a mother who is exhausted and has no more tears expresses her brokenness in this manner, surfaces from the depths of pain and tries to stand up to it."[9] When a twenty-four-year-old died in a traffic accident, his mother danced around his coffin. "It was in no way a joyous act, but the expression of deep pain. She was not willing to acknowledge the death of her son and her deepest wish was for people to celebrate his marriage. Great joy and deep grief are so closely related that the boundaries are sometimes blurred."[10]

Men beget, but women give birth to new life and thus perhaps have a different relationship to dying. Today this is changing before our eyes; children can be produced independently of the rhythm of life, of menopause, and in the world of the affluent there is already almost a feeling of entitlement to postpone death. Until now what birth and death have had in common was simply people's experience of allowing them to happen. Both giving birth and dying give one access to the passivity that is part of life. Expressed in religious language, this passivity was described in phrases like those in the book of Job: "Naked I came from my mother's womb, and naked shall I return there" (1:21).

In our culture people have learned something that is not to be taken for granted in other cultures, nor was it historically taken for granted in our own: That one gains one's own world only through activity, by doing, by giving shape to things. But that is an ambiguous art that we have conquered for ourselves. The aspect of freedom in it is the fact that we are no longer passive sufferers of our fate. We no longer need to bow in silent agreement to everything that is and comes our way. People have become doers. They have learned to see through the laws that govern processes, to overcome distances, to have influence, to see through roles people play, to obliterate diseases, to prolong life. They have learned to be makers of their own lives and fates in a way that was still unthinkable a few generations before.

This obsession with activism brings with it its own kind of misfortune. Peoples' gifts of pathos, those having to do with suffering, accepting, patiently bearing, and enduring, begin to atrophy. People lose their capacity to accept life, to admit limits, to "praise" life, as tradition calls it, even its fragmentariness or even in one's brokenness, that is, to regard life as meaningful. Those who have learned to live life in the action mode, who find justification only by doing, cannot cope with situations in which there is nothing they can do anymore, when limits impose themselves on them as doers. Can doers stand to be powerless? Can they preserve their humanity in life's defeats, if the meaning of their being is limited to activity and the reproduction of life? Can they be sick? Can they die? Or are sickness and death now only to be considered sites of dramatic absurdity, best never thought of at all, to be overlooked or denied? The denial of defeats and limits is desirable in the consumer society. Death has no place in the landscape of doers' and winners' lives. This is why dying is so difficult for us.

As long as we have no other postures toward the world and toward ourselves than that of winners and doers, as long as we hold fast to the imperial interpretation of life, there can be no weakness that could contain a message for us. Then sickness and death point to nothing; they are absurd, without any blessing. They remain enemies, and we never learn that we are fragmentary and that our meaning is not only located in our activities. But perhaps it is possible to hear contradictory voices when faced with pain. Protest and submission, rebellion and affirmation, revolt and humility—I like to use this old-fashioned word—belong together. As strange as it sounds, they can become brother and sister.

Studies in the history of religion have shown that all religions originated in the cult of the dead; they involve themselves with the dead and work on this decisive experience of the limit. For example, there are particular customs in relation to the dead, such as bringing them food for their journey to the next world, remembering the dead, naming their names, uniting the living and the dead as a way of practicing mortality. We need all this. And it is precisely this role that women in almost all cultures have assumed, practiced, nurtured, and performed. The fact that, according to Hippocrates, the medical doctor must have nothing to do with dying and must avoid the house of the dying, speaks a clear language. Their care is left to women.

There is a kind of unity of the dead and the living that used to be taken for granted in all older cultures. The aboriginal population of Bolivia, the Aymara, still continue the ancient custom of bringing food to the dead on All Souls Day each year for three years after their death. It is a family festival, a way of honoring the dead and at the same time a ritual of remembering.

This manner of facing death is absent from our culture, so that the barbarism, this spiral of violence that we are experiencing right now, should not really come as a surprise. Religion's role is to remind people of limits, to give them practice with limits, to arouse consciousness of the limits of natural existence, not to deny these limits. Religion counters our culture's technology-crazed delusions with reminders of the true limits of life and life experience.

At a peace gathering[11]

We're not only ten thousand I said
there are more of us here
the dead of both wars
are with us

A journalist came and asked
how I could know that
haven't you seen them
i ask the clueless guy
haven't you heard your grandmother
groaning
when they started it up again
do you live all alone
without any dead who drop in
for a drink with you
do you really think
you are only yourself

Religion also says that we are open for God, for transcendence, for love. "Nothing can separate us from the love of God."

That we are capable of love is a basic idea that has often been obscured by Protestantism. In the face of all the confessing of sins, we often failed to notice that we are actually able to love, that love can be learned, that it does exist, even in our lives.

Finitude and eternal life belong together in a profound sense. We ought not to split them apart.

This is precisely what the old teacher named Death communicates to us. He teaches both loving and dying. He teaches us how to walk and to love the One who does not pass away.

Saying Good-Bye

When I think about farewells, I spontaneously think of two poems that have been with me for a long time. Looking up these texts from the first half of the twentieth century, I begin to struggle with them, and perhaps my discontent with what are no doubt "great" poems is itself a sign of a certain difficulty that I will never stop having.

> *As every flower fades and as all youth*
> *Departs, so life at every stage,*
> *So every virtue, so our grasp of truth,*
> *Blooms in its day and may not last forever.*
> *Since life may summon us at every age*
> *Be ready, heart, for parting, new endeavor,*
> *To find new light that old ties cannot give.*
> *In all beginnings dwells a magic force*
> *For guarding us and helping us to live.*[12]

The poem is called "Stages" (*Stufen*) and first appeared in the novel *Magister Ludi: The Glass Bead Game*. The author, Hermann Hesse, was sixty-six then. The poem belongs to the tradition of classical contemplative poetry; the iambic meter flows without faltering, the end rhymes embrace one another and resound. The vocabulary—phrases like "stage of life" (*Lebensstufe*), "new endeavor" (*Neubeginn*), "virtue" (*Tugend*), "magic force" (*Zauber*), "cosmic spirit" (*Weltgeist*), "hour of death" (*Todesstunde*)—is characteristic of an exalted literary style. The prevalent attitude is one of imparting wisdom. Each verse culminates in a sententious dictum, such as "We must prepare for parting and leave-taking / Or else remain the slaves of permanence."

I ask myself why this text is no longer helpful to me. In fact, it makes me suspicious in some places. One reason may be that the wisdom expressed here had its rightful place in a conservative life context, in opposition to stubbornness, self-repetition, and a narrowing and enslaving homelessness. Gaining self-assurance through repetition of what "always was" a certain way does in fact require interruption of routine, saying good-bye and breaking away. In the context of conservatism, the poem objects to rigid, encrusted forms.

But in a postmodern era these old fetters of traditional ways are long gone. Flexibility and mobility are long since established values, prerequisite to functioning at work. Obviously, the rapid acceleration of the exchange of consumer goods, which in turn multiplies productivity, also changes our relationship to "life-stage partners," as the expression goes in contemporary German usage. So today, lines from Hesse's poem almost sound like travel agency commercials: "Serenely let us move to distant places / And let no sentiments of home detain us."

But such discomfort is due not only to the half century that separates us from Hermann Hesse's poem. It is also related to the all-too-smooth, all-too-simplistic language of the poem. When it says at the end, "So be it, heart: bid farewell and become well!"[13] this reader, not unaffected by the hermeneutic of suspicion, asks herself whether someone had been ill or what; whether the transitional stages of life alluded to here have not been declared at the outset to be stages in an ascent. I am afraid the poem embodies the bourgeois subjectivity of the industrial world's belief in progress. What I used to hear as comforting words of reassurance—"And life may summon us to newer races"—now seems to me to come dangerously close to the ruthless optimism of natural scientists standing outside any sense of accountability. Now I am taking my critique too far, but the poem is at least vulnerable to abuse, and it can be put into service by the white male who is accustomed to a position of dominance. The serene "distant places"—without limits, without injury, without defeat—can degenerate into a horrific vision. This subjects the transitions of life to the tyranny of so-called positive thinking; they must be read as happiness, widening of horizons, enrichment. If you suffer despite all this, it is your own fault.

The second, poetically stronger poem begins with the admonition "Keep ahead of all parting." It is one of the "Sonnets to Orpheus" (II, 13) by Rainer Maria Rilke.[14] While I have never been able to fulfill the demands of this admonition completely, they accompanied me for a long time.

Keep ahead of all parting,
as if it were behind you
like the winter that is just now past.
In winters you are so endlessly winter, you find
that, getting through winter, your heart on the
whole will last.

Winter, winter, winter, and getting through, last-ing—the poem deals with death and transcendence. The Latin prefix *trans-* means "over, across, beyond, to the other side of." The fact that Rilke bends the trivial phrase "on the whole" into the last line of the second verse of the sonnet shows how important this vocabulary of transcendence is to him. We can, as the text assumes, be "ahead" of parting, of say-ing good-bye, can anticipate our farewell. We can bring it into the presence of the beloved other. This is explicated in Rilke via the myth of Orpheus, who descends into Hades to bring his beloved Eurydice back to earth.

Be ever dead in Eurydice—, arise singing
with greater praise,
rise again to pure relation.

Among the fleeting, in the realm of declination,
be a resonant glass that shatters while it is
ringing.

Death and transcendence intermingle, and time, this slowly ticking clock of our life, is disempowered. Everything is now. Death is taken into the present time of the living in such a way that Orpheus can be "ahead of all parting" and becomes a singer, the origin of all music. The concept that without an inward relationship with death there can be no music is relatively easy to understand. My hesitation, my questioning of Rilke's interpretation of life's transitions, has to do with the relationship to time. "Be ever dead in Eurydice"–Can I do that? Do I want to do that? I thought for a long time about the concluding sentence that then introduces the tercet.

"Be–at the same time, know the terms of negation. . . ." "Knowing" in this context certainly means more than having taken note of something, more than rational knowledge. It must be the kind of knowledge that allows me to be forever dead in Eurydice. The expression "terms of negation" can be related to Orpheus's journey out from the underworld. Persephone forbids him to look back toward Eurydice when he goes to bring her back from the realm of shadows. Orpheus is not able to meet this condition. Dazed by the power of the passionate desire to see his beloved again, and perhaps tormented by the fear that she might not follow him, he turns to look back at her and loses her forever. But this is not Rilke's theme. He wants to take the story elsewhere; he wants to merge Being and Knowing and wants to keep ahead of all parting. And it is precisely here that my doubts grow.

After the death of heinz j harder[15]

I am not through with you
you always made us feel guilty
i always thought it was wrong to look forward
to the weeks when the plums are ripe
to enjoy an orgasm, even the sad kind,
the do-it-yourself kind.
and the boy scout songs of people
who aren't yet ten
i always thought it was wrong
to love all these things
to look for them and let them come
i always thought i would insult you
with my blind love
for something that flits around, fast and elegant
that smells and makes noise
when you bite into it
that sounds and takes me away from here
where i sit around
away, just away from the imprisoned
decrepit i, only i

You lived in your body
bloated by pills
like an alcoholic in a
dilapidated room
you signaled to me
that it is foolhardy and brutal
to laugh and sing and persist
in believing
in the pursuit of happiness
for all

I am not through with you
now you've taken off
from this uninhabitable body
from this useless state

Every life transition has a double perspective: looking back and looking forward. Is it the task of therapy and pastoral care to guide one's view toward the past into a view toward the future? I do not know how to answer this question; what is important to me is to preserve both directions. There exists a polarity between commitment and freedom, between saying good-bye and departing, between the process of breaking off, with all its pain, and what Rilke conjures up in the Twelfth Sonnet with the line "Will the transformation. Be inspired by the burning flame."

I want to hold on to this polarity. I do not want to be "ever dead in Eurydice," because I consider that a betrayal of commitment, of the farewells and the pain that are part of living. Isn't there in Rilke's poetry, or more accurately, in Rilke himself, a tendency to claim freedom without commitment, transcendence that sacrifices immanence? Isn't there a tendency that wants transformation at any price when it claims that "scheme-devising spirit, which masters earthly laws" (II, 12)? I would like to call this a masculine tendency because it opts for freedom, because it does not consider the other, because of its illusion of being autonomous. Total fascination with the view into the future destroys the perspective for looking back to one's pain and renders one-sided the polarities of freedom and commitment, transcendence and immanence, masculine and feminine, in favor of dominance by patriarchy. No, "Be ever dead in Eurydice" is an imperative that promises to master life's transitions and farewells at another, next stage, but its cost is an act of violence, a rape of the other. No, I am not keeping ahead of my parting, not to mention of endless winter. Winter lies ahead for me. I do not want to skip over it or rush ahead to pass by it. I live not merely in becoming, but rather in the flow of becoming and passing away.

Now I want to try to express this again, more clearly, in the language in which I feel at home, the Bible. After all, it constantly deals with life transitions and with immanent transcendence. The two great symbols it uses for brokenness, pain, departure, and liberation are called "Exodus" and "Exile," "Setting Out" and "Expulsion."

Exodus is the setting out of Israel "out of the land of Egypt, out of the house of bondage" (Exod 20:2). The Jewish Seder liturgy says the following about this first, original transitional stage of life: "In every generation human beings are obliged to imagine they themselves departed from Egypt. . . . And you shall tell your son and your daughter on the same day, 'It is because of what the LORD did for me when I came out of Egypt'" (Exod13:8). God did not merely save our forefathers and foremothers, but us as well. "He brought us out from there in order to bring us in, to give us the land that he promised on oath to our ancestors" (Deut 6:23). This is why we are obliged to give thanks, to sing praises, to laud and glorify the One who has done all these miracles and led us

> *out of bondage into freedom,*
> *out of sorrow into joy,*
> *out of darkness into light,*
> *out of bondage into liberation.*
> *So let us sing to him a new song:*
> *Halleluja.*

I, too, have departed from Egypt, and I, too, live by the Exodus and understand the other great symbol of my religious tradition, the Resurrection, in light of this setting out. Much of my theological task, that of developing a theology of liberation for Europe, consists of looking for signs of the transition in which we leave behind the Egypt in us and around us. We need rites of passage, not only for the natural transitions in life, but especially for the work of liberation that is happening in some places. Peace workers who go to Bosnia, tax resisters who refuse to fund the Euro-Fighter combat aircraft any longer, young people who lie down in front of trucks carrying nuclear waste to prevent them from going on—we owe these people, at the very least, a ritual of blessing, of accompaniment, of celebration of life, a ritual that cannot be distorted in the house of servitude.

Exodus means a break, setting out, leaving home. "Now the LORD said to Abram, "Go from your country and your kindred and your father's house to the land that I will show you" (Gen 12:1). Abram is to give up the land, his most important possession aside from the cattle, and likewise his social relationships throughout his clan and neighborhood. Everything that offers security—possessions and family—Abram is to leave behind. The destination is unknown. "Into a land that I will allow you to see" is how Martin Buber renders the promise. Perhaps it is a midlife crisis after settling and becoming rooted in something that had no permanence after all. The setting out of which Exodus speaks is close to the other fundamental motif of the Bible, that of exile and expulsion. Perhaps it was not so easy at all for Abram—who was not yet called Abraham—to tell the difference between exodus and exile. One of the difficulties with life transitions is that feelings of home and feelings of homelessness can exist in one and the same heart. We should learn to pay attention to both.

You asked me for something

You asked me for something
your voice was firm and
your articulation clear
you spoke like someone
who has thought things over
and knows
what they want

You asked me for something
and I had thought you had forgotten how
to ask for something and to hear

me when I ask you
i had thought we were as good as dead
for each other
because we couldn't ask each other for
    anything anymore

Mystery of faith
to ask god for life every day
to hear god asking for life every day

We cannot live without memory. If people think it is possible to live without it, they suffocate something within themselves. People who know no homesickness are missing something. People who make themselves feel so at home here and now that they are indifferent to the homeless all around us do not understand that home and homelessness are part of the same thing.

Religious tradition has stated this very clearly. We are exiled. Our home is in heaven. We were driven out of Paradise; what is here cannot possibly be all there is. Some people hear this and think of a later life that is to begin only after death. But Jewish and Christian biblical tradition is not hooked on the beyond. What it does, though, is make human beings feel they are not completely at home here in the world. Rather, they are in some sense alien in their own country. "I am a guest on earth; here I have no place to stand / Heaven shall become my lot, there is my fatherland," says the hymn (*EGB* 529).

Today utopias are considered obsolete; a kind of swaggering pragmatism prevails. A sense of what is doable seems to triumph over a sense of what is possible. Those who continue to feel like strangers in their own country because they find the air poisoned, the laws against foreigners too inhumane, and the military budget a crime in disguise against starving peoples, are part of a conscious minority. They do not want to be so sold on their homeland, so smugly nationalistic. They remember their country's dark history. The literal meaning of the English verb "to remember" is to become a member again of a family, a group, a people, to blow off the however brilliantly colored and persistent tendencies of our culture toward isolation, to belong to something, to have loved ones, not to stand all alone. We remember Zion, the city of God; so this means that we become a member of this community, with citizenship rights outside our own fatherland. This does make one feel a bit homeless in Gelsenkirchen, Berlin, or Hamburg!

Today we can learn about this from many consciously Christian residents of what used to be East Germany. Did we go through everything we did just to become like people in the erstwhile western Federal Republic? This is what many of them ask. Didn't we have quite different dreams and hopes in those Monday evening peace prayer services and the nonviolent protest marches and at the already forgotten Roundtable?[16] Didn't freedom also mean for us liberation from the human cancer called the military? Didn't reconciliation also mean living at peace with our mother, the earth, instead of plundering her even more skillfully? When we wished for bananas, did we also want porno films and xenophobia? In any case we still have plenty of reason to remember Zion, our homeland. "If I forget you, O Jerusalem, let my right hand wither!" (Ps 137:5).

A master of longing describes in Isaiah 35 the homeland to which he wants to go: "The wilderness and the dry land shall be glad, the desert shall rejoice and blossom" (v. 1). This is the way he dreams of his homeland even as he and his people are in bondage in Babylon. He longs for a land in which he has never been. He lives in exile, deported, driven out of his homeland of Jerusalem. Babylon had a higher culture, had its own alphabet and its own literature, a highly developed legal system, a thriving economy. In Babylon there were rivers of water, unlike his homeland, which was often threatened with draught. And yet this exiled man longs for home, for Jerusalem. He wants to go to the city where the blind see, the lame man leaps like a deer, and the dumb have found speech again. He longs for the land where the desert bursts into bloom and the narcissi grow on the withered steppes, where people no longer tear each other apart like the lion tears its prey. He sees a holy path before him: "No lion shall be there, nor shall any ravenous beast come up on it; . . . but the redeemed shall walk there. And the ransomed of the LORD shall return, and come to Zion with singing" (vv. 9-10).

What does this man want? Who is he, anyway? What city could we recommend to him, and what land would be right for him? Where did anyone else ever restore speech to the dumb? I think this person, this woman with huge desires, sits on the banks of the many rivers of Babylon, on the Rhine, on the

Elbe, on the Volga, and on the Mississippi. She is considered unreliable because in every country her wishes are too great. Everywhere she looks for the dumb who have found their voice again and who are being heard. Everywhere she keeps her eye on the desert that is watered and made fertile. Every city is to her a cage, whether Stuttgart or Hong Kong, and she is never imprisoned in the language of people because the language of her wishes lives on. At home she is in a no-man's-land where no human being has ever been. Every person is a foreigner to her, just about everywhere, and every person of longing is a foreigner, everywhere.

Back then the Babylonians called out to the Jews in exile, "Sing a song of Zion." But they didn't want to sing in Babylon; they didn't want to act as if they were at home there. They held fast to their homelessness for the sake of another home; they understood that even a well-furnished prison is still a prison, and even a democratic army still exists for killing and dying, and even the gentle voice of a commercial means a seduction to lying and denial. Thus longing makes ordinary wage earners into people who say, "We are the people."[17] Religion makes hardworking underlings into unpredictable dreamers, and it is none other than God who makes us homeless where injustice is the rule. Isaiah called the Babylon model "bondage" and was not willing to be talked out of his homesickness for justice. "No," he said, "here we have no lasting city, but we seek the city which is to come" (Heb 13:14).

Give me the gift of tears god[18]

Give me the gift of tears god
give me the gift of language

Lead me out of the house of lies
wash away my upbringing
liberate me from my mother's daughter
take down my protective wall
raze my intelligent walled fortress

Give me the gift of tears god
give me the gift of language

Cleanse me of keeping my mouth shut
give me the words to reach those near me
remind me of the tears of the little
student in goettingen
how can I speak when I have forgotten
how to cry
make me wet
don't hide me any longer

Give me the gift of tears god
give me the gift of language

Dash my pride to bits make me simple
let me be water that people can drink
how can I speak when my tears
are only for myself
take private property and the desire for it
away from me
give and I will learn to give

Give me the gift of tears god
give me the gift of language
give me the water of life

Toward Overcoming Enmity

Taking care of the sick and dying is something that, in our society, is done for the most part by women. Women's attitude and behavior toward death have been described and reflected about in ever-new ways in the past few years. Dying and loss have moved ever closer together, and Rilke's plea—"O Lord, give every man his own death"—seems less and less adequate to me. How do we master death in life? How can we integrate death into our life again instead of repressing and denying it? What does acceptance mean, and when, where, and how does enmity end?

Feminist theology presents a great resource in this connection, particularly in its systematic reflection. Two of the most important fundamental concepts of feminist theology that have helped me to clarify my thinking are "power" and "mutuality." The two are closely interrelated. One doesn't need to have read a lot of Freud to know which part of humanity was so very invested in building up the concept of the "omnipotence" of God! In feminist thinking, good power, which we can also call God's power, is always power that is shared, passed around. It empowers others. "Power is empowerment"—this is a feminist principle, and all power that a man or woman wants to possess and secure for him- or herself is in any case not the power of God.

But to claim this we need a different understanding of mutuality, relationality, and human relatedness. This central principle of systematic feminist theology replaces the concept of dominance or rule that is rooted in sexist thinking. Mutuality is a different kind of relationship than that which we describe with the word "rule" (*Herrschaft*). The fact that the realm of God (*Reich Gottes*) is described with a word from the world of kings (*basileia*) does not justify reducing it to dominion, as happens, for example, in Karl Barth's translation, "God's royal reign" (*Königsherrschaft Gottes*). But this is what has happened in the dominant theological interpretations. A just relationship among human beings as well as between God and humans needs different forms of interaction. The basis for these forms seems to me to be rooted in the personalism of Jewish thought, for example in Franz Rosenzweig, Martin Buber, or Emmanuel Levinas. The relationship between human beings is not to be understood merely as a possibility that is realized now and then. On the contrary, we must conceive of it as *arché*, as the origin, as the "In the beginning" of the creation story. "In the beginning" was relationship (Martin Buber). Neither the lonely *I* nor the lonely divinity is the foundation point of feminist thinking, but the capacity for relationship, the relationality in the process of which both God and human beings become who they are.

Ivone Gebara, a leading Brazilian theologian, writes about the concept of relatedness: "It contains the challenge to understand ourselves anew, again and again, as human beings who, along with other such beings, are part of a single web of life."[19]

This concept is characterized "more by living relationships of fundamental mutual dependence than by hierarchical, pyramidal relationships in which everything seems to depend on a single powerful figure. . . . The human being thus consists first of all in relationship, then consciousness, then personal creativity."[20] "Relatedness points us toward a justice of interdependence and an ecological justice, that is, a justice that includes the ecosystem."[21] The concept of mutuality contains a different kind of intimacy with creation.

"To be fallible is what makes human nature what it is, as it manifests itself in our historical and cultural reality. In fact, this vulnerability and fallibility is precisely what makes us dependent on one another and allows relatedness to become apparent as a constitutive element of our being."[22]

God becomes incarnate, is born anew in the world, and human beings act in accordance with God's will by making justice and love real, in order to bring God into the world as incarnate reality. This process, which feminist theologian Carter Heyward calls "godding," is only possible with mutuality. It includes two elements: dependence, neediness, needing the other in order to come to life, and liberating creative energy, vitality that is needed. I need you, and I am needed. You need me, and you are needed. We are capable of relationship, and we are relational beings who need relationship.

Mutuality is more than merely giving and taking in the sense of enlightened self-interest. The enlightened self-interest that forms the basis of capitalism leaves the giving and the receiving parties substantially unchanged. Mutuality is much more—mostly because the liberal understanding of exchange ignores the question of power. In the process of mutuality, by contrast, the question of power is asked and answered not in terms of dominion and superiority, but through sharing, through the miracle of the "empowering of the five thousand." Good power is mutual power; it gives others a share in the power of life, which is what the concept of empowerment means. To think of God as power-in-relationship means also to understand that any power that we—or others—use in such a way that we do not empower each other is an abuse of power. Traditional theology did not achieve mutuality because it viewed God one-sidedly as a creating, sustaining, giving, judging power. The relationship between God and human beings was interpreted according to the patriarchal relationship of the sexes: active and passive, creating life and receiving life, commanding and obeying, or angrily refusing obedience. For a long time theology articulated God in what seemed to patriarchal thought to be the highest values: king, general, victor, judge, father. These images preclude genuine mutuality, even if they articulate a partial truth. Thus good traditional theology always countered the partial truth dialectically by also speaking of God as servant, prisoner, accused, and sufferer, even as mother (for example, Martin Luther). But this dialectic is insufficient for thinking through genuine mutuality.

A major problem in contemporary churches is that they do not treat people as adults, because they only articulate this one-sided relationship. "God is good; he protects us, warms us, comforts us," is preached and acted out in many languages. I knew a kindergarten teacher who taught a slightly disabled child, "You are totally wonderful. Next week you'll be able to jump as high as the others. And besides, you have the most beautiful hair. That's because God loves you." This kind of encouragement is wonderful; it is a major empowering moment for the child. But it is insufficient by itself. These are one-sided statements that unconsciously become false if they cannot be made reciprocal, if this child does not at some point come to know that "God needs me" as well. I should keep God warm, because God can get really cold when God looks at this life we have here. I can and should love God. It's a puzzle to me sometimes how such a clear statement as the First Commandment, "Thou shalt love God above all things," is forgotten. Our dependence on God is not the biological dependence of a child—in the case of the infant, absolute dependence—on its parents. It is "voluntary dependence," which Goethe calls the "most beautiful state." "And how would this state be possible without love?"[23]

The spirit of the times idolizes the independence of the individual, asserts we are autonomous, sufficient unto ourselves. But is that sufficient for happiness? Real relationships among human beings are always characterized by counting on one another, needing one another, by codependency that asserts voluntary dependence. We are simply smaller, stupider, and uglier without love, and the deeper our relationship to the Other is, the better we know what is meant by the folk song that goes, "I can't live without you, I can't be without you." Maybe I can eat or "enjoy" or have fun, but I cannot "be." I do not need to bake the bread of my life, give myself my own life's energy, be my own comforter. I must not just be myself and realize my own self. Such a basic assumption of individualism in isolation from others, as we all know, destroys the earth and other living beings. Voluntary dependence corrects our fixation on autonomy and self-realization; at the same time it warms us. Kierkegaard writes, "To need God is the highest human perfection." But God needs us as well, our protection, our comfort, our warmth. We need to be needed. Heinrich Böll once said on Good Friday, "Now is the time to comfort God."

Feminist theology proposes a kind of thinking about God that necessarily leads toward a new kind of mysticism. It proposes that God waits for us to appear, asks for our truth, without our courage staying stuck in the cold grief of the universe. It says that God wants to be saved, that is, that even a concept like that of salvation must be thought of in an ethical and theological context of reciprocity. Unilateral relationships in which one person is always the giving one and the other always the receiving one are morally intolerable and lead to neurotic distortions. That is why the image of parental love for God's relationship with us is insufficient. We must become friends of God—this is a Quaker expression that I love very much. Friendship allows us to overcome the infantile image, especially of women in relation to God, that patriarchy

dictates. When we have successfully separated ourselves in our relationship to our parents, the result
is friendship based on mutual need. When theology
separates itself from patriarchal ways of thinking, it
also rejects its own infantilism.

This is exactly what women in many places in
the world are working on today. The groaning of
creation can scarcely be ignored anymore; it has
called forth a new form of feminist theology.[24]

In her essay "Why Death?" Ivone Gebara writes
about what she learned while studying theology:
"To conquer Death, to conquer this peculiar kind
of thief who robs us of life! To kill Death! This is
what I learned, without really understanding what it
means."[25] But this is exactly what is not helpful in
"our suicidal, genocidal, eco-cidal society" that takes
the death of other living beings in stride as a matter
of course. Gebara's hope, which can take away our
cold fear, is my hope as well. "I believe it is possible to integrate death more firmly into our being,
as a part of us that belongs to everything living."[26]
Rubem Alvez calls upon religions to stop killing
death—as he puts it mockingly—"so that there is no
dusk left in the world, so that the sun is always high
in the sky." This victor mentality does not help us
move forward. It denies finitude and transitoriness
instead of accepting death "as a reality in myself,
as a spiritual space,"[27] in which I can receive and
love other transitory things. If there were not death,
"how could we speak about being born?" Every song
we sing comes and goes. Every summer evening is
transitory, not forever. But our transitory nature is

not our greatest misfortune. It is from our oldest teacher, Death, that we learn that "for everything there is a season" (Eccl 3:1). The circular motion of the earth, the rhythm of life, is a condition for what we call love. "It is death that makes room for us to know that things are transitory." The mentality of the affluent world, the "all things at all times" mentality, makes love impossible. This also makes death and love inseparable from each other; they go together "like two tender conspirators."[28]

The language of Ivone Gebara becomes more and more poetic in this text about death because she comes closer and closer to mysticism, and that always means closer to its ineffability. Mystical language attempts to say the unutterable. The acceptance of death is not denial of its pain or of the fact that it is unbearable. Instead it is an attempt to include it in the rhythm of created life. Without death we could not enter into the "circular motion of the earth."

The piety that is finding expression here is not so much one of salvation as one of creation. "Death, holy death, is a part of life, interwoven with one's own life. It is part of the same thread and therefore it is beautiful . . . a mysterious, sad, and great beauty."[29] This is one way to express the acceptance of finitude, which is at the same time carried by a love of what is eternal.

The Death of My Mother

My mother died in September 1990.[30] She had turned eighty-seven that summer. The last nine nights and eight days I spent at her deathbed in my parents' house. At first she did not recognize me, but she held both of my hands firmly with her dry, bony hands. She gesticulated and groaned deeply or cried out loudly for "Mama," "Papa," for Strasbourg, the city of her childhood, and sometimes for her grandchildren, my children. When I stood by her bed, I started talking about whatever came to mind. "It won't be long now. It's a dark tunnel you have to get through. At the end it will be light. Don't be afraid! I'm staying with you now. The tunnel is awful; it's too narrow, but then it will be broad and bright."

While talking like this I would think about how often my mother, who had given birth to five children, compared death with the labor and pain of childbirth. It was an idea that seemed to calm her— death as a task that one has to finish. I didn't know whether she took in anything I said; certainly my touch and my subdued but firm voice calmed her.

Then it occurred to me to sing, because words no longer got across. I sang "*Befiehl du deine Wege*" ("Commit Thy Ways to God," *EGB* 361), a hymn she liked and one that one of my daughters had recited to her for her eightieth birthday. I sang the three or four verses I knew by heart, then I added other songs and some liturgical responses like the one from Taizé, "*Laudate omnes gentes, laudate dominum*" (Praise, all people; praise the Lord). Whenever I didn't know the words, I hummed the melody again, loudly and clearly. My mother became calmer and fell asleep.

In the nights and days that followed, I sang hour after hour. I got myself a hymnbook and looked up the verses I didn't remember. In so doing I discovered that many hymns include references to death even when they deal with dawn breaking or the quiet of the forests. When I got to the verse *"Der Leib eilt nun zur Ruhe / legt ab das Kleid, die Schuhe / das Bild der Sterblichkeit"* (The body hastens now to rest, throws off its garments, shoes, its image of mortality), my mother nodded and stretched her feet; it often gave her relief to kick off her shoes. I did not know how much of the following she heard or even believed: "I'll take them off / and Christ will clothe me with the robe of honor and glory."

But everything I sang seemed to be relevant. Her feet were blue and swollen, but the hymn writer Paul Gerhardt knew more than this to say about my mother's feet: "The one who gives clouds, air and wind, their course will also find paths where your foot may tread." Mother, who would often cry out for air, heard the word "air" clear as a bell.

Far clearer than my prose was the language of the hymns that was often associated with memories of other people. Thus I even sang the sentimental song "So Take Now My Hands" in memory of my godmother, who was a deaconess at the Bethel Institutes.[31] She died over fifty years ago and was the first dead person I consciously saw as a child. The verse "Wrap me wholly in your mercy" brought to

our minds—or perhaps only to mine, who knows?—
the great blanket of evening, night, and death.

What was I doing, then? I was inviting the dead
whom my mother had loved to be present with her.
I spoke the name of my brother who had died while
a prisoner of war. With the dead, the past returned.
I also sang "Dear Moon, you drift so quietly through
the evening clouds," a song that she had recently
sung to her great-grandson because of its tender line
"Beam lovingly into the quiet little room of those
who are troubled."

My mother was a child of the nineteenth century even though friends sometimes called her
an eighteenth-century "lady." Her relationship to
church and piety was only a matter of form; in the
last years of her life, it was even cool. A phrase
she would use to distance herself from religion and
faith was "We don't know that." It amazed me how
often she folded her hands during the nearly four
weeks of her death struggle. As if crying out loud
were not enough.

Every now and then I also recited a psalm,
the 23rd, about the good shepherd, and the 126th:
"When the LORD will release the captives of Zion, we
will be like those who dream."[32] Yet it almost seemed
to me as if the foreign words of the Latin prayer calls
touched her more deeply. During the times I would
sing to her, I had a feeling of connection with her,
as if she found contentment through the singing.
It was not as if I was doing something "for her,"
but as if we were together and were walking toward
something greater than we are. An old theological

conviction of mine was strengthened during these nights at her deathbed—namely, that without mutuality, without giving and taking on both sides, love is not possible; and further, that God cannot "give" us anything if we do not become bearers and givers of God's power.

The singing and praying that are still alive in the culture of Catholic villages are helpful in the time of transition both for those who are actively engaged in their own dying and for those accompanying them. "Swing low, sweet chariot," I sang, as much for Mother as for myself, "coming for to carry me home," as if we all stood at the Jordan where Christ replaced the ancient, ominous ferryman, Charon.

The physician and the various family members had announced frequently already that her death was near. And how often she herself had wished for it during the past year! She had often told an anecdote about the death of President Hindenburg, who had asked his physician, Dr. Sauerbruch, "Herr Professor, is Friend Hein in the room yet?" and was told, "No, Your Excellency, but he's at the door." With such stories she expressed that she was becoming comfortable with dying. Indeed, she was expressing her wish to die, which she had only recently admitted but then articulated more and more clearly.

But her energy to live was stronger than her conscious awareness. She still wanted to do so much—to sit up, get more air, be turned over, have something to drink. For an entire day she called out, "Turn over!" in a complaining, demanding, imploring voice, as if words like "Help," "Mama," "Turn over," and "Out" all had the same purpose even though assigned to different days. Often she would leave language even further behind and would answer only with a nod or a shake of her head. Her arm and leg movements had become smaller.

The first evening with her I had hardly been able to finish singing the verse "When my time comes to leave," because I had begun to cry. The last evening I sang it quietly, and when I came to the verse that says, "Appear to me, be my image, my comfort as I die," I thought of the many different images that arise during the process of dying, from childhood, from the fear of being left alone.

The names of her grandchildren came more often to Mother than those of her own children. Should we cling to images—like that of the light at the end of the tunnel? Are they needed, either by us who die passively or by those who actively seek death? If death is the quintessential condition for which there is no image, is it possible to dress it up with images and thus to humanize it? Can death come, as Matthias Claudius—and Schubert—put it, as a "friend, and not to punish"?

The last hymn I sang was "Lord, Have Mercy." My mother had begun to breathe regularly again, though rapidly, for the first time in a long while. I had put my hand on hers; her face was completely relaxed. Her last sigh was light like an amazed "ah." For a moment I doubted the presence of what had been awaited for so long. But it had stepped into the room.

What Is Salvation?

Do humans need salvation from death? Is finitude our primary misfortune? The "Our Father" in the Christian liturgy attributes to God eternity, as well as sovereign reign, power, and glory. Perhaps the greatest wish that Christianity has articulated is that we might be able to participate in these three promises during our earthly life: in the reign of justice, in the power of indelible hope, and in the glory of love—perhaps even better, in the beauty of love! But is this intended "forever and ever," even for mortal human beings?

I think Rosemary Ruether is right in assuming that women are less interested than men in "denying their mortality with the help of doctrines of a life after death." Isn't there an underlying denial here of the body that is seen as unimportant? And are women not different because they have a different relationship to giving birth? The category of "natality" or born-ness to which Hannah Arendt drew our attention is perhaps more compatible with mortality. Ruether asks the hard question whether the longing for immortality is "not the height of male individualism and egotism." "What separates us from God is not our mortality, but our killing. When Paul connects sin and death, what he means is the killing of our fellow human beings—and today, our earth. Death is a part of life, but not the premature and violent death from which we profit."[33]

I wonder whether we are promised individual life after death. In the Revelation to John, so-called natural death is never mentioned. "It is not death that is to be abolished, but killing, murdering, lying, and exploitation."[34]

The hope for resurrection is characterized not by modern individualism but by the apocalyptic tradition. It is not about the continuation of the life of the individual person or about any rewarding of good people as individuals.

It is about a new heaven and a new earth that come about with the coming of God and God's justice. The earth is the place of transformation, and this takes place, to use the metaphors of the apocalyptic tradition, in the collaboration between God, who takes the role of "the most experienced of all midwives," and Mother Earth, who gives life. "The transformation of the unjust world into the world full of life in full bloom is compared with the labor of giving birth. . . . It requires the participation of Earth and its inhabitants. With this eschatological gynecology it becomes possible to articulate a human-divine cooperation." This is a central point of feminist theology, because in the concept of cooperation, there is an attempt to think of God not only as *a se*, complete and independent of us, as in the language of tradition. God should be represented not as "omnipotent" but like any Beloved, relying on and dependent on a Counterpart.

We need not overcome our born-ness. If we think of it in connection with our mortality, then our relationship with death could more easily shift to one of acceptance, freedom from fear, and affirmation. If we can perceive and affirm God's immanence in our lives, in other words, if we experience holiness because God takes place in our lives, then that can be experienced in our dying as well. "God happens"—that for me is a fundamental statement, more important than any "proof" of the existence of God. This can be true in living and true in dying.

Perhaps the language of theo-poetry is stronger here than the language of theology. An American friend sent me this poem:

> *Do not stand at my grave and weep.*
> *I am not there; I do not sleep.*
> *I am a thousand winds that blow,*
> *I am the gleam of diamonds in the snow.*

The author sees herself in the calmly circling birds and the gentle shine of the stars at night, and ends with the words:

> *Do not stand at my grave and cry.*
> *I am not there; I did not die.*[35]

According to this text, we are able, in dying, to enter into creation, we belong to creation, are part of its coming and going, its coming again and leaving again. We are no more than the wind, the sunlight, the snow.

But can this suffice to describe one's love for a human being? Heinz Roehr, a Quaker friend, sent me a haiku about the questions I have been struggling with:

> *To love someone*
> *Means to say: Despite decay*
> *You will not die.*[36]

But am I not my body? It is the memory that keeps me alive for a certain period of time, best expressed in the Bolivian ritual of bringing food to the cemetery for the deceased man or woman every year for several years on All Souls Day. The Bible expresses this in the image that we are "written into the Book of Life." God is memory, and in this sense God's eternity is also the eternity that we do not possess, but in which we can participate.

American women friends told me about a festival in a rural commune in which a dying woman took part. She listened to the music and saw the people dancing in the great hall where the festivity was taking place. One person after another came over and sat down with her and visited with her. She was not alone. It was a death that had nothing to do with guilt, shame, or denial. God can be present in time and space even when our time on earth is coming to an end.

We should learn to accept becoming and passing away.

> *The roses die*
> *Without pleading for grace.*
> *They let themselves gently float down*
> *To caress the earth.*

This poem by Horst Hirchmeier is entitled "Transitory."[37] It is an affirmation of this earthly existence, which always means a transitory existence, and at the same time, it affirms its recurrence. Is not my wish for this creation to remain alive much greater than my wish that I myself remain alive?

Mark Twain wrote a humorous little book purporting to contain the diaries of Adam and Eve. Under the title "After the Fall," the only entry is an excerpt from Eve's diary. Similarly, after the entry "Forty Years Later," there is a reflection on death: "But when one of us must leave first, I ask that it be me. For he is strong, I am weak. He does not need me as much as I need him. A life without him would be no life for me—how should I bear that? And this longing, too, never goes away and will not stop voicing itself as long as my kind, womankind, walk the face of the Earth. I am the first woman and I will be born yet again when the last woman is born."

Adam had one more thing to add, an inscription on Eve's grave: "Wherever she was, there was Eden."[38]

chapter four

Your Steadfast Love Is Better Than Life (Ps 63:3)

Gerhard Tersteegen: A Mystic of Death

Gerhard Tersteegen (1697–1769) was a mystic of the Reformed Church; as a pietist and a layperson, he had huge difficulties with that church all his life. His father died when he was young, in 1703. While his mother managed to send her extraordinarily gifted son to the Latin School in Moers—he was frail and plagued with illness throughout his life—her means were insufficient to allow him to study theology. He apprenticed with his brother-in-law, a merchant who was as brutal as he was successful; then he even tried for two years to run his own business. At age twenty-two he gave that up in order to work in solitude as a weaver of silk ribbons, a starvation job, spending ten to twelve hours daily sitting in a bent-over, cramped position at the loom.

On Maundy Thursday in 1724, Tersteegen had a conversion experience, ending his "dark years" and opening the door to the revival movement, the "Awakening." This is recorded in a "dedication" to Jesus that he prepared in the manner of the French Quietists and wrote with his own blood. "To my Jesus! I dedicate myself to you, my only savior . . . to be utterly and eternally your possession. With my whole heart I renounce all my rights and whatever power I have over myself. From this night forward, my heart and all my love I surrender and sacrifice forever to you as the gratitude I owe. Your will be done, not mine, from now on to eternity. Command, govern, and reign in me! I give you complete power over me."[1]

Some years later, Tersteegen gave up his trade, began to write, and worked chiefly as a pastoral caregiver and director of revival meetings but also as a lay medic administering herbal remedies and tinctures. He began to write pious works and spiritual reflections, for example a collection of rhymed sayings with the humorous title "The Lottery of the Pious." Later, many of his hymns found their way into hymnals. He became well known in pietistic, often separatist circles and could barely keep up with the many invitations, including those of wealthy patrons in Holland. He lived frugally in a pilgrim's hut in the vicinity of Duisburg; the greater part of the food brought to him he took to the homes of the poor in the evening. His writings became known rapidly. Even Frederick the Great got his hands on them and, while traveling to the town of Wesel, invited the pious and highly intelligent author for a conversation. As so often before, Tersteegen had to decline for reasons of health.

The Reformed and Lutheran Churches were especially irked that the father of the revival movement in the Lower Rhine regions spent twenty years composing biographies of Catholic saints. The twenty-five men and women, Francis of Assisi and Teresa of Avila among them, were shining examples to Tersteegen, but his attention to them discredited him as a "papist" with Catholic leanings.

In a letter of thanks for birthday greetings, he described "the three kinds of birthdays of God's children." The first is the physical birth where the child "cries right properly." It is followed by the second birthday: baptism, which is understood as a rebirth, where the child "is transported step by step from the narrow and dark condition of nature into the light of grace." The third birthday is our physical death; Tersteegen knew how closely connected death and birth are. Dying "releases God's children from this frightened world, from the narrow prison of this humiliated body, from every pressure and danger to the soul because they are right joyfully born and taken into the wide space of dear, sweet eternity." One must not fear death and "the brief birth pangs," but the children of grace must "indeed also moan and cry until they get through." "At this birth, the angels stand ready to take the children born into blessed eternity into their arms and carry them to God's bosom."[2]

What was this pious believer's understanding of eternal life? When asked, "Where is heaven?" he replied in his *Geistliches Blumengärtlein* (*Spiritual Flower Garden*):[3]

> *Don't ask where heaven is, depart from your*
> *   own self,*
> *else, wherever you are, heaven will remain*
> *   strange, far away.*
> *Whoso dies to his own will and can give*
> *   himself to God*
> *will on earth already dwell with God in*
> *   heaven.*

Classical mysticism repeatedly described this giving over of the self in the medieval phrase "Go out of yourself"—*gang uz dir selbst uz*.[4] Such forgetting the self, "becoming unattached" (*entwerden*) to one's self, finds ever new, drastic names in Tersteegen. "It disgusts me to see myself. My actions are soiled, my thinking, willing, and understanding are full of self."[5] To be dependent on God alone: that is the manifestation of ultimate freedom. Only in dependence on God can freedom from all things, from cravings and needs, be attained.

> *Destroy, O Lord, all that of self,*
> *eradicate the "mine"*
> *May your dependent way of Life*
> *fully in me shine.*[6]

Here death is understood as the liberation from the ego. In his instruction on prayer, Tersteegen tried to teach people that God is not "our lackey."

"Begging" or "demanding" are replaced by an intimacy with God, expressed in sentences like these: "I do always pray, yes, but not with my mouth," "having nothing but God in all," "desiring nothing," "able no longer to do anything on your own, to be nothing: that is the greatest teaching."[7]

Later Tersteegen wrote "A Believing Soul's Thoughts on Dying."

> *Step by step I walk toward great eternity,*
> *unnoticed fades life's short span. . . .*
> *You, God of eternity, who gave me life,*
> *I give it back to you with all I am and have.*[8]

There is no talk anywhere in this kind of mystic yearning for death about life continuing after death, about reunion or the immortality of the soul. Tersteegen wants to be "in God." He desires no immortal or infinite ego; unlike Goethe, he does not desire to leave "a trace of my earthly days" in the aeons and in that sense become "eternal." Faith in eternity plays a significant role, but it is not a faith in the ego continuing to live; it is, instead, being kept in God. "O Eternity, so beautiful, attune my heart to you, my home is not in this time."[9]

For Tersteegen freedom means to be free of fear, of worries about physical well-being or economic destitution. True life takes place in remembering God instead of in the state of being where God is forgotten, which he passionately fought against and which has become so utterly normal in our world.

The days when you're forgotten
are like something thrown away;
then none can be contented,
for heart and life you gave
to us for you alone;
in none but you is there rest.

One of the clearest mystical expressions is in the hymn "Gott ist gegenwärtig," "Lo, God Is Present," or "God Reveals His Presence," in the fifth verse in Tersteegen's text.

Air that filleth everything,
wherein we always hover,
of all things ground and life,
ocean without ground and end.
Wonder of all wonders,
I sink myself in Thee,
I in Thee, Thou in me,
let me wholly disappear
and see and find Thee only.[10]

But must "I" disappear so that I find "Thee"? Our language is often clearer than we ourselves know. Rapt with enthusiasm and happiness, I can exclaim things like: "When I heard that movement of the cello concerto, I was totally blown away!" What a wonderful state when I am so happy that I am absorbed, "disappear" as Tersteegen says, become free of myself.

This is the language of the love of God, it is the language of mysticism, of the thirteenth-century love poem: "I am thine, thou art mine, of that thou canst be certain." It is a language that makes itself disappear. I no longer belong to myself, am no longer "the human turned in on her- or himself," as Luther defined the sinner. To be in this love of God is to be free. Tersteegen, the mystic plagued by illness, did not long for death; he yearned for God. "Away pretence and dream, away creature! For the One alone do I desire to live."[11]

chapter   five

Where Love Is, There Is God

WHEN I THINK OF THE concept of "love," the first thing that comes to mind is a medieval hymn.[1] Having been revived by the movement associated with the Taizé Community, it is often sung today. *"Ubi caritas et amor, ibi deus est"*—where love is, there is God. Not veneration of God in humility and devotion, no adoration of a higher being beyond our comprehension is at the heart of religion, but love in the two-fold sense of this word that portrays us as those who are loved and as those who love. To believe in love means to experience ourselves as affirmed, desired, and accepted beings and, simultaneously, as those who themselves become love. To become able to love is life's aim. When tradition speaks of "eternal bliss"—a term often misunderstood today—it means simply that love and justice show their power—in everyone, for everyone. The curious coupling of *amor* and *caritas* (Greek *eros* and *agapé*) in the hymn referred to is at the very core of the Christian religion. In antiquity, the word *eros*, meaning "yearning" or "desiring," designated a demon that could drive human beings beyond themselves into fulfillment and completeness. *Eros* is rooted in the feeling of incompleteness, the lack of and the yearning for what is not now and yet not only "should" be but actually also "wants" to be. This erotic power lives in all human beings in that they are oriented toward—or, more accurately and in the language of piety—are "created" for relationship.

When early Christianity wanted to describe its central understanding and its praxis of love, it did not draw on the concept of *eros*, but chose the much more inconspicuous word *agapé*. It came from the tradition of the meal shared in brotherly/sisterly fashion, known as "communion" or the "*agapé* meal." There, *agapé* meant people ate together, sharing what they had, in the feast of faith: slaves and masters, women in the textile trade unable to get rid of the stench of animal skins, store owners, Jews and Greeks, locals and people from away. The meal was the concrete expression of their togetherness; the love meal bonded them one to another. For them, the human body was not a bothersome nuisance that interferes with the ascent to what is higher, but it belonged right in the midst of the new, liberated life.

Later, in theological reflection, church fathers and bishops tried to make a clear distinction between love from above and love from below. The former was said to emanate from God; the latter, at its best, was to reflect God but also to exclude all sexual connotations as much as possible. From its very outset, the Jesus movement rejected this separation of "divine" love from "earthly" love. More than the other gospels, the Gospel of John narrates "love stories," as Luise Schottroff calls them, that tell of Jesus and his relationships with people such as Mary, Martha, Lazarus, and the beloved disciple, John, without inhibition about the erotic element. These are wonderful examples of the creative power that comes to light where what we call *eros* and *agapé* have become one.

"Whoever does not love does not know God, for God is love" (1 John 4:8). In this brief sentence, "God is love," the New Testament provides its only definition of the undefinable God. And here the two very qualities of love are present, namely giving and taking, becoming and making new, giving life and becoming alive. They are indivisible. Here, the patriarchal understanding of sexuality, which splits genital sexuality off from the great web of our bodies' and souls' relationship with other human beings and the world, has no place at all.

Agapé is the ability of the ego to abandon itself. Jewish philosopher of religion Martin Buber expresses this basic given of human existence like this: "In the beginning was relationship." We are not simply the being who has a knack for trade, for whom it is enough to pursue self-interest; we need more for life than that. "In the beginning" there was not the "homo oeconomicus," this individual able to do business and to seek pleasure that we are to be made into these days; rather, in the beginning there was the self-transcendence of love.

Being loved awakens our ability to love. But is religion really needed to understand that? Isn't rational analysis enough? Doesn't psychology provide what is necessary for working through the parent-child relationship? To what extent is more needed than that? Isn't *religio*, "reconnecting," at least in its institutionalized form, more a crusty web encasing this glowing core, something distracting rather than upbuilding? I think that our ability to relate needs a language that is more than that of argument. The mystery of life that people from the most diverse religions have called the Eternal, the Triune, Allah, energy, the power of goodness, the Ineffable—this mystery wants to be shared.

"God is what is of all the most communicable [*das Allermitteilsamste*]," Meister Eckhart says.[2] This sentence often throws me. I despair because it often seems absolutely impossible to communicate even the least of that mystery. Religion grows from the necessity of finding a language that goes all out, that imagines and evokes more that what can be read off and produced.

It is in the interest of love to focus on the need for a language that connects us with others and with a tradition that transcends pure subjectivity. We are all "incurably religious," as Nicolai Berdyayev put it. Leaving this illness behind us is at the same time one of the tasks of God's *eros*, without which life does not live. My doubts about people who believe themselves "cured" of this illness and have therefore "no truck with religion" have steadily grown in face of our totalized economic system. Can we really live without "the love of God that surpasses all our understanding"? Isn't the renunciation of religion a renunciation of *eros*? To say of someone that she or he is "unerotic" is to me tantamount to a death sentence. The destruction of our other wishes and dreams for the life of all creatures on this planet continues with the marginalization of religion. Is not what many regard as a kind of enlightened intelligence much rather akin to the clinical term "treatment (of the illness of 'religion') successful—patient unfortunately dead"?

I ask myself sometimes why there is so little language of God's love in of all places the Christian affirmations of faith. Instead, there is most often only a pallid talk of a Lord-God who loves and protects us little creatures and who doesn't expect a thing of us. I see one of the causes of the weakness of institutionalized religion in the world in people's religious desire to remain in the role of a child for as long as possible, indeed forever. This frantic clinging to childhood is infantile and has nothing to do with the wide-open, amazed eyes of the children that Jesus had in mind. Growing into adulthood, against and at the same time along with the institutions of religion, means above all taking love seriously in all its mutuality. Angelus Silesius's verse "I know that without me God could not live one moment" is a mystical expression of this mutuality, contrary to every orthodox concept of a rigidly hierarchical "above" and "below."

The "reign of heaven" the gospel speaks of has something utterly different in mind. It wants us to participate in that reign where the last shall become the first. We are to love the Eternal One through having part in her/his being. The clearest expression of this in the New Testament is in the writings attributed to John. He is regarded as the apostle of love and traditionally represents the mystical element of the Christian religion. The Quakers, modern-day mystics, speak of "that of God in us"; it is really nothing other than the radical embrace of the Jewish core commandment that relates to the love for God. "Therefore, love Him, your God, with all your heart, with all your soul, with all your might" (Deut 6:5, in the translation of Martin Buber).

What kind of love is that? I would like to focus on two points that are important to me. The first is the holistic sense that speaks here. You are to love God "with all your heart, with all your soul, with all you can do." When do we ever do something "with all," without reservations, without an "if" or "but," without expecting recompense or punishment, without constraint or the deadly "and then what?" that kills the present moment? When do we ever experience something that becomes a pure "now," and when are we fully what we are doing? "I am what I do" is a classic mystical formulation for this wholeness. In love, being and doing coincide. When do we attain that centeredness and that undistracted attentiveness that are inherent to love? Thich Nhat Hanh, a Buddhist monk, formulates this same core way of being in these words: "Wash dishes in order to wash dishes."[3] It is an act of undistracted dedication; it presupposes the individual's ability to relate to the Whole. The ego is not the final horizon of the self. We are able to leave ourselves behind, become the cloud we see passing overhead, the song we are singing. We are not only the limited and predictable product we often turn ourselves into. In the beginning was the relationship that constitutes us. We exist "in the accusative," as Emmanuel Levinas put it; we are addressed, breathed upon, beheld, and needed. Being whole signifies the delight of "behold!"

For me the second indispensable point in any reflection on love is mutuality. It is the nature of love to renounce the differentiations between giving and receiving, acting and being acted upon, dispenser and receptacle, active and passive. Love seeks to assert the unity of acting and receiving gifts. The act of giving the self that binds us to something greater than the ego cannot be described only in concepts rooted in the sexual experience of one half of humanity.

But love does not think only in interpersonal terms; it lives in structural attentiveness to reality as well. It is inseparably bound to justice—which is one of the great strengths of the Jewish and the Christian tradition. Love's political name is justice. More and more human beings suffer from our economic system. More and more human beings suffer from our ecological condition. Lacking measures to intervene on behalf of the most powerless and for their protection, and without declaring work a human right, this market economy offers no model of humaneness. It can function for a segment of the world's affluent people only. Presently more than 75 percent of all countries are organized according to our system of neoliberalism, while in nine of ten countries people go hungry and are allowed to die of hunger. Does the market have nothing to do with that? It knows no needs, only demands; that is its principle of operation. Those who have nothing to offer to meet this demand are dead. For need itself is not marketable.

For God, however, the needs of human beings are most important; needs have priority for God over productivity and performance. Today God still hears the cry of her people, just as she heard their cry in Egypt long ago. "I have heard the cry of my people." God is the one who knows our needs and lives wherever we hear with his ears.

"God has no hands but ours," writes Teresa of Avila. To love God does not mean to abandon responsibility but to share it. The best translation of what the early Christians called *agapé* is still "solidarity." And it is solidarity that is in grave danger among us because love of neighbor is held to be a private hobby and not thought of in structural terms. Love for justice remains harmless because our stories of justice lack substance, because in our world free of religion and void of tradition, our memory of getting out of rich, slave-holding Egypt has faded. A little bit of fairness—the current euphemism for economic justice—is all that we can conceive of anymore.

When conceived of in terms of religious tradition, interpersonal and structural love requires not only occasional feeling; it also needs to be acted out. There need to be stories; love has to be told, played, danced, sung, and whistled. Love withers away in the speechlessness of a world where everything can be acquired, paid for, produced, and where the absence of genuine at-home-ness in this world—more than an object to be used—becomes ever more tangible. Love needs nourishment that traditions and stories provide; when love is missing or injured, this must be acknowledged and named. Love has to be evoked over and over again. God is not "private property."

A teaching of the Jews is that we are to imitate God, that there is an *imitatio dei*, a discipleship of imitation. As God made clothing for Adam and Eve when they had to leave Paradise, so we are to clothe the naked. God buried Moses, and thus we too are to honor the dead and bury them. God gave bread to the hungry widow in the story of Elijah, and so we also are to imitate the power of God and feed the hungry. God forgives us humans our debts; why then can we not forgive our debtors (such as the hungry people of Nicaragua)? The notion that it is the market that we are to venerate as the ultimate and definitive entity that orders all things contradicts this perception of human life, which manifests its resemblance to God in this discipleship of imitation. God needs us for his reign. The image of God as an unmoved, tearless lord who needs no one in order to live is bad theology fraught with dogmatic conceptions. Nothing has enticed me into Christianity as much as this conviction: God needs us.

The greatest danger I see spreading among us is a spiritual matter: that we think of ourselves as incapable of action and thus remain fixed in the feeling of our own impotence. Perhaps nothing separates us from love as much as the anthropological pessimism that has no confidence in love, because it doesn't know that love gives expression to "that of God in us." There is nothing more godless than saying, "There's nothing we can do about it; that's just how it is." Such thinking denies our bond with God, with the power that holds out to the end, arises again and again, and pleads the case of life for all that lives. This enduring power is not one of supranatural intervention, for God is not an "interventionist" but an "intentionist" whose will we can know: life is for all.

One of the chief tasks of religious connection with the whole human family and with the life of all brothers and sisters is to give expression to our life's intentions, to our wishes. Religion helps us renovate our wishes, not to relate them all too narrowly to the achievable, to what is possible now. It binds together what is isolated. Its most important language is prayer, the kind of wishing that does not simply settle for what is now. Love needs this language, which transcends the realistic, the probable. Love of neighbor, of the world around us, is held in the love of God. In this kind of wishing, God is not an idol of fate in whose power everything happens the way it happens. Instead, it allies us with a god who is not the omnipotent victor but who is on the side of the poor and disadvantaged. This is a god who is still hidden in the world and who seeks to become visible.

"Nothing can separate us from the love of God," Paul writes in his Epistle to the Romans (8:35). We cannot taste this deepest certainty when, like children, we want to wrap God's mantle around us and then, when we grow into adulthood, think that we can do without it. It is simply too cold in the world to believe that we can live without that mantle. God's grace does warm us, yes, but at the same time it makes us help to knit the mantle.

The curious experience of an otherworldly fate turning into living together here below was depicted long ago by a Muslim person of faith. The mystic Bayazid Histami had made a pilgrimage to Mecca and visited the House of God containing the Holy Rock, the Kaaba. He said, "For a while I circled around the House of the Kaaba. When I came to God I became aware that it was the House that encircled me." Searching was changed into being found, and the acceptance of dogmas and teachings became a mystical life with God. Out of the helplessness where we can only submit to God or discard him as a premodern illusion grows a different strength, that of being at one with God's love. We believe that it is we who circle around the house, but in truth it is the house that encircles us and we have long since been inside it.

At Home in This Cosmos

I BELIEVE IN LIFE AFTER death, the life that continues after my individual death.[1] I believe in the peace that will perhaps exist someday when I am long dead; I believe in justice and in joy. I do not believe in a continued individual existence, and I would not want to get into a situation of having to believe in one. That feels to me like a faith-crutch, while in reality we are intended to learn to walk.

A young woman once asked me, "Do you think everything is over when we die?" I replied, "It depends on what you mean by 'everything.' If you are 'everything' there is for yourself, then everything is over for you. If not, then everything lives on." As a lovely Yiddish song puts it, *mir läbn ewig* (we live forever).

The existence of the individual and of the mind (*die individuelle und geistige Existenz*) ends with death. The idea that I am a part of nature, that I fall down like a leaf and rot, is not an idea that instills terror in me; the tree continues to grow, grass grows, birds sing, and I am a part of this whole. I am at home in this cosmos.

Where Are We Going?

Human beings do not live by bread alone. In fact, we die from bread alone, an omnipresent, terrible death. Death by bread alone is the death by mutilation, death by suffocation, the death of all relationships. Bread alone guarantees the kind of death where we can continue to vegetate for a while because the machine is still running, the terrible death by lack of connection: we continue to breathe, keep on consuming, we eliminate, we get things done, we produce, we still mutter words, and yet we are not alive. . . .

To be alone and then to want to be left alone, to have no friends and then to mistrust and despise people, to forget other people and then to be forgotten, to have no one to live for and to be needed by no one, to fear for no one and not to want anyone to be concerned for you, no longer to laugh or be smiled at, never to cry or be cried over—this is the terrible death by bread alone.

My neighbor, an elderly, childless gentleman who had lost his wife several weeks before, called to me to come outside so he could show me that the children had leaned their bicycles up against the fresh layer of stucco on his house. "Look at that scratch!" he said. "Just look at it! After all, property is all we have left in this world!" People die from bread alone. My neighbor worked for his house, lived in it, rented it out, renovated it, protected it; property was, "after all, the only thing we have left," and I saw and heard that he was dead. His horrible death consisted in having no relationship and no connections with other people.

This is the death of which the Bible speaks. The person for whom other people do not signify wealth, challenge, or happiness, but only fear, threat, competition. The person who lives from bread alone and dies of it, of the bread you cannot live on. This is the death the Bible speaks of; it fears this death and arouses the fear of it—not the exit we mostly associate with death, but the death that is a senseless and empty life, the death amidst absence of relationship, fear, speechlessness, abandonment. In a psalm the abandoned speaker cries out, "I must dwell among the dead." He envisions himself as death itself, laid in the pit, dwelling in darkness, misery, without friends.

> *I am counted among those who go down*
> *   to the Pit;*
> *I am like those who have no help,*
> *like those forsaken among the dead,*
> *like the slain that lie in the grave,*
> *like those whom you remember no more,*
> *for they are cut off from your hand.*
> *You have put me in the depths of the Pit,*
> *in the regions dark and deep. . . .*
> *You have caused my companions to shun me;*
> *you have made me a thing of horror to them.*
> *I am shut in so that I cannot escape;*
> *my eye grows dim through sorrow.*[2]

Pain isolates us, deadens us to feeling, destroys the communication that is necessary to survive. As the psalmist experienced pain, sickness, and defeat, so we experience death by bread alone. This is the death the Bible speaks of: this horrible death in the midst of life, running in neutral, boredom, functioning in such a way that living becomes mere existing and human beings degenerate into working beasts. This is the death the Bible speaks of: The prodigal son lives alone in a strange land, he takes care of another man's pigs, he works for starvation wages. He lives only for bread and he lives by bread alone. Thus his father says of him, "He was dead." He lived without relationship; he could not speak with anyone. His labor was used; in this way he vegetated on without any hope for a change in his condition. This is not life, says the Bible; one cannot call this life, this condition of functioning on and on. The prodigal son is still breathing and working, but this existence among the swine is not something you can call living. Living would be different; this is being dead in the midst of life. This is the judgment of the father in the story, this is Jesus' judgment; let us also learn to judge like this. "To survive is not to live," wrote the students in May 1968 on the walls in Paris. Going on, surviving, elbowing one's way through, this is not life. This is the death that threatens us.

"Mitten wir im Leben sind, mit dem Tod umfangen" (In the midst of life we exist surrounded by death) (*EGB* 518). We do not need to think of cancer and automobile traffic here, nor to accommodate ourselves to a consciousness that life is transitory, for

that is a matter of pagan aesthetics. The death that really threatens us, that surrounds us in the midst of life, is the death in the absence of connectedness. It is not taking leave from a stage of life that is difficult for us; for many, it is even impossible to find a moment in life when words like "farewell" and "pain" still have meaning. Absence of connection, the state of death that rules in and of itself does not even allow the bittersweet feeling of individual pain to arise. This is the hell that swallows us up in the midst of life, in the midst of the process of production. Death is the "wages of sin"; that is, the consequence of pseudo-living, death from absence of connection and of fear of one another, death from a life that was nothing but surviving, death from bread alone.

The reason we die by bread alone is that we live for bread alone. This death is not natural but violent; it violates the living. It is a death ordered and organized by the violence of the structures under which we live and willingly accepted by our own addiction to choosing to kill and be dead over exposing ourselves to the dangers of being alive. These dangers are extraordinary: whoever is alive, whoever is still moving, still touching others and being touched, runs the risk of going crazy in a society that lives for bread alone and subordinates everything to profit. Here I am speaking on behalf of the growing number of people in care facilities and treatment rooms whom we call mentally ill or emotionally disturbed because they resist omnipresent death. Vicariously for us healthy ones, who continue to play the game, they embody a kind of life, or rather an outcry for the sake of life, in a world dominated by violent death. They are Abel and they are being conquered. The first death the Bible speaks of is a killing, an act of getting the other person out of one's way. Cain eliminates Abel. In that ancient story it is violence to one person, but in our world violence has become structural, anonymous, and overpowering.

Bertolt Brecht writes, "There are many ways to kill. You can stick a knife into someone's belly, you can withhold their bread, refuse to heal their illness, stick them into poor housing, work them to death, drive them to take their own life, send them to war, etc. Only a few of these are against the law in our state."[3] We can add any number of things to the list of different ways of killing people: You can rob children of their childhood by forbidding them to move or make noise; you can lock them up with forty others and forever destroy their joy in learning and their curiosity to discover things. There are many ways to kill. One can build apartment buildings and plan cities so that even in the smallest possible space as little contact will occur among people as possible. One can always put a Greek next to a Turk, next to a Serb on the assembly line of foreign workers so that no communication takes place and the production process is not disrupted. There are many ways to kill. One can intimidate foreigners with bureaucratic red tape for so long that they take their own lives. One can configure the environment in production, administration, or schooling so that people function without bumping shoulders and develop as little contact with one another as possible.

For unlike the young man in the story of the prodigal son, people do not willingly or unthinkingly leave for a strange land without any connection in order to feed another's hogs, but are instead sent there by the orders of structural violence. The absence of connection that the Bible calls death is ordered and practiced in the most important area of life, namely the area of work. To be dead is something we learn; we are trained to exist as dead people. The dismemberment of life into recognizable, controllable, but at the same time meaningless fragments equals becoming used to the death that is handed to us from childhood on. This is the death the Bible speaks of. If all interests are subordinate to the interest in increasing profit, then every other interest in life is trivialized: You can take them or leave them, be for or against them; one can be more interested in the homeless and another in sports cars; one likes animals and another children; one likes the Adriatic and another the North Sea. . . . Life is a great supermarket; you can have anything, but there are no longer any reasons to be particularly interested in a certain thing. If you relate to all things as a consumer, then relationships can only go as far as they do with things one can buy. Today many people experience the world as a supermarket; they push their shopping cart through the aisles with concentration and at the same time absentmindedness. Death by absence of connection rules the scene. The average citizen of Germany watches TV for four and a half hours per day. Where is one supposed to practice relationship, spontaneity, working for a cause? The world is a supermarket and a factory, of bread alone and for bread alone; we are dying the daily death of this bread.

It is this death of which the Bible speaks. It calls this death "the wages of sin" or "the last enemy." Jesus organized resistance to this death. The stories of the raising of dead persons like Lazarus or the little daughter of Jairus deal with battling the acceptance of death. They call us to resist death; they encourage us to believe, and that means to take sides with life. It is made known to us that death's dominion is being overcome, not only in the resurrection of Jesus, but also in the stories told from his life. Where violence and lack of connection are the rule, death rules. The more we live without connection, the more we acknowledge and tolerate death's dominion. What does Angola have to do with us, though it is German weapons that bring death to Angolans? What does black infant mortality in the Union of South Africa have to do with us, although it is our stock market investments that increase in value thanks to the exploitation of blacks and this kind of death! To be uninvolved, to want to live free of pain, to function only for bread and to live by bread alone, to tolerate violence and contribute to its existence, to love the order that guarantees the continuation of these conditions—all of these things comprise the way we have arranged our life. It is a love for everything that is rigid and orderly, reduced to a number, a love that the psychoanalyst Erich Fromm called "necrophilia," the lustful commitment to everything that is dead, ordered, recognizable, without spontaneity or wishes.

Necrophilia dominates not only the life of the state and of bureaucracies. Our children, too, are defined by necrophilia. The highest value is accorded to what is ordered, registered, dogmatically fixed, posing no risk to canon law. The Christ who is loved is the "honey-sweet Christ, pleasing to our murderous nature," as Thomas Müntzer put it 450 years ago. This honey-sweet Christ guarantees our affluence and eternal life as an extra bonus. He doesn't interfere with the arms industry and offers the assurance of meaning for our humdrum existence to boot. In this necrophilic orientation to life, people honor as God a being whose most important activities are "maintaining," not creating, "controlling," not changing, "protecting," not liberating, a nonpartisan being that resembles a computer, loaded with data about human beings. But the God of whom the Bible speaks is partisan. This God took sides with life, against death, against death by napalm, death from hunger, death by bread alone, by choking to death.

Believing in God means changing sides in favor of life, ceasing to be complicit with death. It means letting go of the drive to kill and the apathy that comes so close to that drive. It means letting go of the fear of dying and the fear of coming up short, two fears that look so alike they are easily confused. . . . To take the side of life means not remaining neutral between murderers and victims, not regarding the world as a supermarket where one can buy this and that and everything as long as the bill looks right and everything is kept in order.

Jesus radically took up the cause of life and fought against death wherever he encountered it: the death of the lepers who were cut off from communication and never touched, the social death of the tax collectors who were regarded as nobodies like the guest workers in our society, and the physical death of those who had not yet lived. But we must observe something here that is essential to understanding Jesus' relationship with death. People like Jesus and his friends who fought against the violent death that is created by human beings for other human beings, whether social or physical death, did not view their own dying as the worst thing that can happen to a person. They feared a life ruled by death more than death itself. They found it worse to live under the deadly rule of death by oppression and choking that is created by human beings for other human beings than to die. Their greatest enemy was not natural death but the violent, creeping death, that kind of being-without-life, that we see every day in the faces of so many people in this society. This kind of dying and this kind of death—by bread alone and for bread alone—deserves the utmost resistance, deserves passionate struggle.

But our relationship with death is exactly the opposite from that of Jesus and his friends. We stick to the honey-sweet Christ and do not want the bitter Christ. We accept more or less as fate the violent death that is all around us, death as a social event, death from wars, from malnourishment, from stupidity, the choking death by bread alone, the daily horrible death of not-living-at-all. On the other hand, we fight with immense effort against natural death, the hospital death of the individual, as something preventable. Acceptance and more or less agreement are the order of the day when faced with the ever-present, slow death by choking, while we battle and protest against the natural and private event of natural death. This battle and this effort are reflected in our death notices, where even the eighty-year-old has died "suddenly," "unexpectedly," or "unfathomably." It is as if no one knew what they were letting themselves in for by living. Sex education and a permanent state of preparedness through information, knowledge, and technical options like the pill are reflective of a seemingly childish state of unpreparedness for death, for it may not be anticipated, known, or discussed. There are old people's homes where talking about death can get you discharged; mentioning dying or naming one who is dying is undesirable and can be punished by the loss of one's eligibility for a room in the facility. Doctors and nurses contribute in their work to allowing death to be taboo; they cannot tolerate death in the realm of their work, perhaps as a reflex of their denial of their own death. The fear of speaking about death, speaking with dying people, looking the fact of dying in the eye, is increasing. We must understand this suppression as a sign of unlived life; the less human beings have lived, have made a real life for themselves, have lived and experienced their emotional, cognitive, and sexual potential, the harder it is for them to die.

One can understand the fear of death as the feeling of an individual that life still owes them something. The person who expresses him- or herself primarily through having, achieving, and consuming must fight death, must suppress and deny it. The denial of death is a form of fear that has been rendered speechless. In the grasp of this fear, people duck to avoid death as long as they live by bread alone and have not become free. The *I* that has not found peace with itself must fight against dying. It only comes to accept dying when physically forced to do so, whereas the purpose of learning about dying for Christians would be to be able to accept death. Here, in the dying of people who have not become satisfied in life, we find the deepest justification for the wish for individual life after death: in the protest against the death of those who have lived too little—not too briefly, but with too little intensity and authenticity. There is nothing that can battle death except love, and that is why the death of people who have never dived into this stream of love is without hope. The only way we can express our taking sides for life—against this death without having lived—is as protest and lament. But we can accept the kind of living that does include death.

No longer having to hate, no longer needing to be afraid, being able to affirm the great Yes that faith signifies, all this includes our learning to die. By living freer from fear, we will learn to die freer from fear. The more we become a part of the love with which we know we are united, the more immortal we are. Speaking in Christian terms, death is always behind us, but love is before us. "We know that we have passed from death to life because we have loved one another. Whoever does not love abides in death" (1 John 3:14). To be Christian means that we *have* passed over into life, we have transcended death. Our path cannot be described in biological terms of first being born, then dying, but the other way around: we pass from death to life. The individual then no longer needs those faith-crutches that are expressed as hoping to see each other again or for a continued individual existence. Nothing can separate us from the love of God, not even the knowledge that our personal existence is transitory. Nothing can separate us from the infinite life into which we have chosen to enter through faith; nothing can separate the drop of water from the stream to which it belongs—not as something superfluous or without essence, but as the essential component of the stream. What would the stream be without drops of water? What would God be without us? What would love be without those who participate in it, who live in it, from it, and for it? Nothing can separate us from the love of God. As people not separated or divorced from this love we live, and can bear to stop being here. We can throw our aggressive energies and abilities at the death of which the Bible speaks, the death from bread alone that makes us choke and lets the other two-thirds of the world's population starve to death. We will be like Jesus was, who stood up to defend the life of others and yet could accept his own death. We are learning to be like Jesus and to leave death behind us. Then our energies are not tied up in the contradictions of fear that we cannot and must not show; they are freed. Then our question is no longer

"Is everything over when we die?" Only those whose ego is imprisoned within the limits of individual existence, who encapsulate themselves to avoid the reality that touches and transforms one, can ask this question. "Is everything over when we die?" is a godless question. What is this "everything" for you, anyway? You [as a Christian][4] cannot describe your own death with the formula, "Then everything is over," because part of what it is to be Christian is not being everything there is for oneself alone. No, everything is not over. Everything continues. Everything I lived for, everything I tried to do with other people, everything I started and everything I failed at—it all goes on. I won't be eating anymore, but bread will be baked and eaten. I won't be drinking anymore, but the wine of brotherly and sisterly love will continue to be shared. I will no longer breathe as this individual, this woman of the twentieth century, but the air I breathed will be there, for everyone.

Against death

I must die
but i'm telling you
that's all
i'll do for death

I'll refuse
all other thoughts
of respecting its officials
of celebrating
its banks as people-friendly
its inventions as scientific progress

I'll resist
all the other seductions
to mild depression
to well-oiled autonomy
to the sure knowledge
that death will win out anyway

I must die
but i'm telling you
that's all
i'll do for death

I'll laugh at it
tell stories
about how people outwitted it
and how the women
drove it away

I'll sing
and regain lost land
from death
with every note

But i'm telling you
that's all

Against cold

When you said put on your shirt
it's cold
i thought i have to die
maybe it'll be another five or ten years
but a death shroud i will have to put on
because it's cold

and we haven't thought of anything yet
to fight the cold
but a little shirt

About resurrection

They ask me about resurrection
sure sure i've heard of it
that a person doesn't race toward death
    anymore
that death can be behind you
because love is in front of you
that fear can be behind you
the fear of being abandoned
because you yourself
i've heard of it
it's, well really
that nothing exists
that could go away forever

O don't ask about resurrection,
a fairy tale from olden days
you can get it out of your head real fast[5]
i listen to the people
who hang me out to dry and put me down
i settle in
to adjust bit by bit to being dead
in my heated apartment
with the big stone in front of the door

O do ask me about resurrection,
o don't stop asking me

works cited

Büchner, Georg. *Danton's Death*. Oxford: Oxford University Press, 1971.

Celan, Paul. "Death Fugue." In *German Poetry in Transition, 1945–1990*. Hanover, N.H., and London: University Press of New England, 1999.

Clemens, Samuel [Mark Twain, pseud.]. *Die Tagebücher von Adam und Eva*. Freiburg, 1994.

Evangelisches Gesangbuch. Frankfurt/Main: Spener Verlagsbuchhandlung GmbH, 1994.

Farhat-Naser, Sumaya. *Verwurzelt im Land der Olivenbäume*. Basel: Lenos, 2002.

Fromm, Erich. *Psychoanalysis and Religion*. New Haven, Conn.: Yale University Press, 1950.

Fromm Forum, no. 3 (1999).

Freiherr von Eichendorff, Joseph. "Moonlit Night." In *European Romantic Poetry*. Edited by Michael Ferber. New York: Pearson/Longman, 2005.

Fünfsinn, Bärbel, and Christa Zink, eds. *Das Seufzen der Schöpfung. Ökofeministische Beiträge aus Lateinamerika*. EMW, 1998.

Gebara, Ivone. *Out of the Depths: Women's Experience of Evil and Salvation*. Minneapolis: Fortress, 2002.

von Goethe, J. W. *Elective Affinities*. New York: Lovell, Coyell, 1882.

_____. "Der Totentanz." In *Deutsche Gedichte von den Anfängen bis zur Gegenwart*. Düsseldorf: August Bagel, 1966.

Gorky, Maxim. "Devushka i Smert." In *M. Gorkii, Sobranie sochinenii v vosemnadtsati tomakh* (*Collected Works in Eighteen Volumes*). Moscow: Gosudarstvennoe izdatel'stvo Khudozhestvennoi literatury, 1960.

Grewel, Hans. *Lizenz zum Töten* (*License to Kill*). Stuttgart, 2002.

Gutmann, H. M. *Mit den Toten leben. Eine evangelische Perspektive* (*Living with the Dead: A Protestant Perspective*). Gütersloh: Bertelsmann, 2002.

Heine, Heinrich. "Don Ramiro." In *The Complete Poems of Heinrich Heine*. Boston: Suhrkamp/Insel, 1982.

Hesse, Hermann. *Magister Ludi: The Glass Bead Game*. Toronto, New York, and London: Holt, Rinehart, Winston, 1969.

Kautzky, Rudolf. *Sein Programm. Neutestamentliche Texte—neu* (*His Program: New Testament Texts, New*). Stuttgart: Media Taschenbuch, 1984.

Levinas, Emmanuel. *God, Death and Time*. Stanford, Calif.: Stanford University Press, 2000.

Lewis, Clive Staples. *A Grief Observed*. San Francisco: Harper Collins, 1994.

Luther, Henning. "Tod und Praxis. Die Toten als Herausforderung kirchlichen Handelns. Eine Rede." In *Zeitschrift fuer Theologie und Kirche* (ZThK).

Luther, Martin. *Luther's Works*. Vols. 51–52, *Sermons*. Minneapolis: Fortress, 1959, 1974.

_____. *Luther's Works*. Vol. 54, *Table Talk*. Minneapolis: Fortress, 1967.

Mankell, Henning. In *Frau und Mutter* 11 (2001).

Mayer, Michael. *Totenwache* (*Death Watch*). Vienna: Passagen Verlag, 2001.

Northwest German Radio broadcast, November 17, 2001.

Plato. *Phaedo.* Oxford: Clarendon Press, 1975.

Rilke, Rainer Maria. *Sonnets to Orpheus.* Berkeley: University of California Press, 1967.

Salomon, Alfred. *Von allen Dingen freier. Das Leben Gerhard Tersteegens* (*Freer of All Things: The Life of Gerhard Tersteegen*). Wuppertal: Aussaat Verlag, 1997.

Schottroff, Luise. "Die Schreckensherrschaft der Sünde und die Befreiung durch Christus nach dem Römerbrief des Paulus" (Sin's Reign of Terror and Liberation through Christ in Paul's Epistle to the Romans). In *Befreiungserfahrungen. Studien zur Sozialgeschichte des Neuen Testaments* (*Liberation Experiences: Studies in the Social History of the New Testament*). Munich: Chr. Kaiser Verlag, 1990.

Schweitzer, Albert. *Werke.* Vols. 3–4. Munich: Beck, 1974.

Soelle, Dorothee. *Against the Wind: Memoir of a Radical Christian.* Minneapolis: Fortress, 1999.

_____. *Fliegen Lernen* (*Learning to Fly*). Berlin: Wolfgang Fietkau.

_____. *Ich will nicht auf tausend Messern gehen* (*I Don't Want to Walk on a Thousand Knives*). Munich: Deutscher Taschenbuch Verlag, 1987.

_____. *Loben ohne Lügen* (*Praise without Lying*). Berlin: Wolfgang Fietkau, 2000.

_____. *Spiel doch von Brot und Rosen* (*Play Something about Bread and Roses*). Berlin: Wolfgang Fietkau, 1981.

_____. *The Silent Cry: Mysticism and Resistance*. Translated by Barbara and Martin Rumscheidt. Minneapolis: Fortress, 2001.

_____. *Verrückt nach Licht* (*Crazy for Light*). Berlin: Wolfgang Fietkau, 1984.

Soelle, Dorothee, and Luise Schottroff. *Den Himmel erden: Eine ökofeministische Annäherung an die Bibel* (*Heaven Down to Earth: An Ecofeminist Approach to the Bible*). Munich: Deutscher Taschenbuch Verlag, 1996.

Sutter-Rehmann, Luzia. "Die Offenbarung des Johannes" (The Revelation of John). In *Kompendium feministische Bibelauslegung* (*Compendium of Feminist Biblical Interpretation*). Gütersloh: Christian Kaiser, 1999.

Ziegler, Jean. *Die Lebenden und der Tod* (*The Living and Death*). Darmstadt: Luchterhand, 1977.

n o t e s

Frontispiece

1. *Do not stand at my grave and weep.*
   I am not there; I do not sleep.
   I am a thousand winds that blow,
   I am the gleam of diamonds in the snow,
   I am the sunlight on ripe grain,
   I am the gentle autumn rain.

   When you awaken in the morning's hush,
   I am the gently rising rush
   Of quiet birds in circled flight.
   I am the gentle stars that shine at night.

   Do not stand at my grave and cry.
   I am not there; I did not die.

The German version of the poem "Do Not Stand at My Grave and Weep" reproduced here in Soelle's handwriting is dated April 24, 2003, Hamburg, three days before her death, presumably translated by Soelle from the version sent to her by an American friend. The English version above is by the Translators, except for the lines Soelle quotes on page 93, above.

Foreword by Fulbert Steffensky

1. See *The Silent Cry: Mysticism and Resistance*, trans. Barbara and Martin Rumscheidt (Minneapolis: Fortress, 2001).

Translators' Preface

1. Dorothee Soelle, *Wo Liebe ist, da ist Gott: Eine Meditation in Texten, Bildern und Musik* (Freiburg, Basel, and Vienna: Herder, 2004). The original publication included a CD of texts, illustrations, and music, spoken by Fulbert Steffensky and Margot Kässmann.

Prologue: Dear Mr. Death and Co.

1. The phrase "black milk of dawn" occurs in Auschwitz survivor Paul Celan's German poem "Death Fugue" (*Todesfuge*), well known to German readers; it alludes to the ashes rising from the chimneys of the crematoria at the death camps. These are overseen by "the master from Germany," i.e., those who meticulously plan and implement the genocide. Cf. Charlotte Melin, ed. and trans., *German Poetry in Transition, 1945–1990* (Hanover, N.H. and London: University Press of New England, 1999), 85–87.

Chapter 1. Old and New Fears

1. Cf. Soelle's chapter "On Forgetting God," in *The Silent Cry: Mysticism and Resistance*, trans. Barbara and Martin Rumscheidt (Minneapolis: Fortress, 2001), ch. 12.

2. Luther, 163, T-U 83 [DS]. (Cf. ch. 4, n. 2.)

3. Ibid., 162, T-U 83 [DS].

4. H. M. Gutmann, *Mit den Toten leben. Eine evangelische Perspektive* (Gütersloh: Bertelsmann, 2002), 92.

5. This is our literal rendition of the German verse cited by Soelle, likely from a recent German translation. The English equivalent of Ps 68:21 in the Luther Bible reads: "We have a God who helps, and the Lord, who rescues us from death." The NRSV has in verse 20 (not 21): "Our God is a God of salvation, and to GOD, the Lord, belongs escape from death."

6. Poem and its source not identified.

7. *EGB* 101, v. 4. We have translated the cited verse literally in order to retain Soelle's emphasis on the mockery of death. This corresponds to the familiar English verse, "O Grave, where is thy victory?" in Paul's First Letter to the Corinthians and in the Bach cantata by this title.

8. Johann Wolfgang von Goethe, "*Der Totentanz*" (The Dance of Death), 1813. Our translation. Cf. Theodor Echtermeer and Benno von Wiese, eds., *Deutsche Gedichte von den Anfängen bis zur Gegenwart* (Düsseldorf: August Bagel), 1966.

9. "Don Ramiro," in *The Complete Poems of Heinrich Heine*, trans. Hal Draper (Boston: Suhrkamp/Insel, 1982), 33–37.

10. Cf. Maxim Gorky, "Devushka i Smert" (Death and the Maiden), subtitled "Skazka" (A Fairy Tale), in M. Gorkii, *Sobranie sochinenii v vosemnadtsati tomakh* (*Collected Works*

in *Eighteen Volumes*), ed. V. Volina (Moscow: Gosudarstvennoe izdatel'stvo Khudozhestvennoi literatury [State Publishing House of Belles-Lettres], 1960), 1:17–23. All cited passages of the 1892 poem are our translations from the German version cited by Soelle.

11. Cf. Dorothee Soelle, *Against the Wind: Memoir of a Radical Christian*, trans. Barbara and Martin Rumscheidt (Minneapolis: Fortress, 1999), 155ff.

12. Soelle cites *Frau und Mutter* 11 (2001), 22.

13. Our translation. The German original, "Ein fest überschreitet mehrere grenzen," appeared in Dorothee Soelle, *Verrückt nach Licht* (Berlin: Wolfgang Fietkau, 1984).

14. Our translation. As with the previous poem, the German original, "Ein anderes verhältnis zum tod," appeared in Soelle, *Verrückt nach Licht*.

15. Hans Grewel, *Lizenz zum Töten* (*License to Kill*) (Stuttgart: Klett, 2002), 97ff.

16. Soelle references Henning Luther. Source not identified.

Chapter 2. Is Death the Last Enemy?

1. On C. S. Lewis, cf. Dorothee Soelle, *The Silent Cry: Mysticism and Resistance*, trans. Barbara and Martin Rumscheidt (Minneapolis: Fortress, 2001), 22–23.

2. C. S. Lewis, *A Grief Observed* (San Francisco: Harper Collins, 1994), 19.

3. Ibid., 41–42.

4. Ibid., 43.

5. Ibid., 42.

6. Cf. *Silent Cry*, 59–60.

7. Lewis, *A Grief Observed*, 85–86.

8. Ibid., 88.

9. Ibid., 94.

10. Michael Mayer, *Totenwache* (Vienna: Passagen Verlag), 2001.

11. Northwest German Radio broadcast, November 17, 2001.

12. Emmanuel Levinas, *God, Death and Time*, Bettina Bergo (Stanford, Calif.: Stanford University Press, 2000), 105.

13. *Silent Cry*, 211.

14. Levinas, *God, Death and Time*, 22.

15. Cf. *Silent Cry*, 211–12.

16. Levinas, *God, Death and Time*, 111.

17. "Tod und Praxis. Die Toten als Herausforderung kirchlichen Handelns. Eine Rede" (Death and Praxis: The Dead as a Challenge to Church Action; A Talk), *Zeitschrift für Theologie und Kirche*, vol. 88, 407–26.

18. No citation given in the original text of DS.

19. Luise Schottroff, "Die Schreckensherrschaft der Sünde und die Befreiung durch Christus nach dem Römerbrief des Paulus" (Sin's Reign of Terror and Liberation through Christ according to Paul's Letter to the Romans), in *Befreiungserfahrungen. Studien zur Sozialgeschichte des Neuen Testaments* (*Liberation Experiences: Studies in the Social History of the New Testament*) (Munich: Chr. Kaiser Verlag, 1990), 59.

20. Ibid., 64.

21. Ibid., 65.

22. Ibid., 62.

23. Rudolf Kautzky, *Sein Programm. Neutestamentliche Texte—neu* (His Program: New Testament Texts, New) (Stuttgart: Media Taschenbuch, 1984).

24. Schottroff, "Die Schreckensherrschaft der Sünde," 59.

25. Albert Schweitzer, *Werke*, vol. 3 (Munich: Beck, 1974), 28.

26. Schweitzer, *Werke*, vol. 4, 166.

27. No page reference given in DS.

28. Schottroff, "Die Schreckensherrschaft der Sünde," 60.

29. Ibid., 60.

30. Erich Fromm, *Psychoanalysis and Religion* (New Haven, Conn.: Yale University Press, 1950).

31. *Fromm Forum*, no. 3 (1999), 39–40.

32. Cf. Soelle, *Es muss doch mehr als alles geben* (There Must Be More Than Everything) (Freiburg: Herder, 2002). [DS.]

33. Cf. Dorothee Soelle, *Against the Wind: Memoir of a Radical Christian*, trans. Barbara and Martin Rumscheidt (Minneapolis: Fortress, 1999), 18f.

34. Jean Ziegler, *Die Lebenden und der Tod* (The Living and Death) (Darmstadt: Luchterhand, 1977), 79.

35. No citation in DS.

Chapter 3. Women and Death

1. "Lord, save yourself!" is Soelle's paraphrase. In both Luther's German Bible and the NRSV, the verse reads: "God forbid it, Lord!"

2. NRSV: "Pray with me."

3. Plato, *Phaedo* (Oxford: Clarendon Press, 1975), 116. The translator of this edition notes that he is using page numbers from the Stephanus edition. In the following, citations are from this edition unless noted as our own translations.

4. Ibid., 117.

5. Our translation.

6. Plato, *Phaedo*, 117 c, d, e.

7. Georg Büchner, *Danton's Death*, act 4, scene 3. We have rendered this more literally than Victor Price in the 1971 Oxford University Press version (p. 62) in order to reflect Soelle's point.

8. Translations of Luther's sermon citations by Soelle are our own.

9. Our translation. Soelle's citation is from Sumaya Farhat-Naser, *Verwurzelt im Land der Olivenbäume* (Basel: Lenos, 2002), 204.

10. Ibid., 205.

11. Our translation. The German original, "Auf einer Friedensversammlung," appeared in Dorothee Soelle, *Loben ohne Lügen* (Berlin: Wolfgang Fietkau, 2000).

12. Hermann Hesse, *Magister Ludi: The Glass Bead Game*, trans. Richard and Clara Winston (New York: Holt, Rinehart, Winston, 1969). Citations in the following are from p. 411 of this edition unless otherwise noted.

13. Our translation. The Winston translation reads: "Bid farewell without end," omitting the idea of getting well or healing contained in the final word of the original, the command to get well (*gesunde!*).

14. Here and throughout this section we cite the English version by C. F. MacIntyre (Berkeley: University of California Press, 1967), 80–81.

15. The German original, "Nach dem tod von heinz j harder," first appeared in Dorothee Soelle, *Spiel doch von Brot und*

Rosen (*Play Something about Bread and Roses*) (Berlin: Wolfgang Fietkau, 1981).

16. Prior to the fall of the Berlin Wall and the East German regime in November 1989, there were weekly Monday peace prayer vigils in many cities throughout what was then the German Democratic Republic. The churches provided the only public space in which open discussion, demonstration, and prayer could take place despite the presence of the state security police. The "Roundtable" refers to the year-long process of meetings in which the newly formed democratic parties met after November 1989 in an attempt to incorporate the ideas of the East German opposition into a new constitution. With the March 1990 elections, these hopes were crushed.

17. "We are the people" (Wir sind das Volk) was the slogan of many East German opposition groups leading to the fall of the Berlin Wall and the nonviolent overthrow of the existing regime in November 1989.

18. Soelle's source list indicates that the German original (untitled) first appeared in Dorothee Soelle, *Fliegen lernen* (*Learning to Fly*) (Berlin: Wolfgang Fietkau, 1979). Cf. also Soelle's *Ich will nicht auf tausend Messern gehen* (*I Don't Want to Walk on a Thousand Knives*) (Munich: Deutscher Taschenbuch Verlag, 1987), 103.

19. This and the following citations are our translations from the German version Soelle had before her: *Die dunkle Seite Gottes—Wie Frauen das Böse erfahren* (*The Dark Side of God—How Women Experience Evil*) (Freiburg, Basel, Vienna: Herder, 2000), here, p. 181. The book is available in English as Ivone Gebara, *Out of the Depths: Women's Experience of Evil and Salvation*, trans. Ann Patrick Ware (Minneapolis: Fortress, 2002).

20. Ibid., 171.

21. Ibid., 181.

22. Ibid., 173.

23. J. W. von Goethe, *Elective Affinities* [DS].

24. Cf. Dorothee Soelle and Luise Schottroff, *Den Himmel erden. Eine ökofeministische Annäherung an die Bibel* (*Heaven Down to Earth: An Ecofeminist Approach to the Bible*), (Munich, Deutscher Taschenbuch Verlag, 1996) [DS].

25. Our translation. Cf. Gebara, *Out of the Depths.*

26. Bärbel Fünfsinn and Christa Zink, eds., *Das Seufzen der Schöpfung: Ökofeministische Beiträge aus Lateinamerika* (*Creation's Sighing: Eco-Feminist Essays from Latin America*) (EMW, 1998), 81. [DS]

27. Source of citations in this paragraph are not identified; translations are ours.

28. See page 12, above.

29. Gebara, *Out of the Depths,* 82.

30. Translation of "Der Tod meiner Mutter," from *Gewöhnen will ich mich nicht: Engagierte Texte und Gedichte,* ed. Bärbel Wartenberg-Potter (Freiburg, Basel, and Vienna, 2005), 103-7.

31. The Bethel Institutes near Bielefeld, Germany were founded in the nineteenth century to care for patients with seizures and various other mental and emotional disabilities. Many unmarried women found careers as deaconesses in such facilities. In the Nazi years, the director, Friedrich von Bodelschwingh, was one of the first to discover and resist the "euthanasia" program that called for the deportation and gassing of the mentally retarded and emotionally disturbed.

32. We follow the Luther Bible here rather than NRSV to emphasize the connection Soelle makes between dying and being released from captivity. NRSV reads: "When the LORD restored the fortunes of Zion, we were like those who dream."

33. DS does not identify source of Ruether quotes.

34. DS reference is incomplete. Cf. Luzia Sutter-Rehmann, "Die Offenbarung des Johannes" (The Revelation of John), in *Kompendium feministische Bibelauslegung* (*Compendium of Feminist Biblical Interpretation*), 2nd ed., (Gütersloh: Christian Kaiser, 1999), 741.

35. Cf. the complete poem in frontispiece note on p. 137, above, translated into German by Dorothee Soelle and written out by hand just days before her death. The lines cited on this page appear in English in Soelle's original.

36. Source not identified.

37. Source not identified.

38. S. L. Clemens [Mark Twain, pseud.], *The Diaries of Adam and Eve* (New York: Samuel French, 1990) [DS].

Chapter 4. Your Steadfast Love Is Better Than Life

1. Alfred Salomon, *Von allen Dingen freier. Das Leben Gerhard Tersteegens* (*Freer of All Things: The Life of Gerhard Tersteegen*) (Wuppertal: Aussaat Verlag, 1997), 45.

2. DS's citation, "T-U, 337," is not explained. (Cf. ch. 1, n. 3.)

3. T-U, 339.

4. *The Silent Cry: Mysticism and Resistance*, trans. Barbara and Martin Rumscheidt (Minneapolis: Fortress, 2001), 213.

5. T-U, 339.

6. T-U, 340.

7. Salomon, *Von allen Dingen freier*, 62.

8. T-U, 340.

9. *Evangelisches Gesangbuch* (Frankfurt/Main: Spener Verlagsbuchhandlung GmbH, 1994), no. 481, v. 2.

10. Ibid., no. 165, v. 5.

11. Salomon, *Von allen Dingen freier*, 132.

Chapter 5. Where Love Is, There Is God

1. Translated from "Wo Liebe ist, da ist Gott" (Freiburg, Basel, and Vienna: Herder, 2004).

2. Cf. *The Silent Cry: Mysticism and Resistance*, trans. Barbara and Martin Rumscheidt (Minneapolis: Fortress, 2001), 97.

3. Cf. *Silent Cry*, 177.

Epilogue: At Home in This Cosmos

1. Dorothee Soelle, *Gewöhnen will ich mich nicht: Engagierte Texte und Gedichte,* Bärbel Wartenberg-Potter, ed. (Freiburg, Basel, and Vienna: Herder, 2005), 90–107.

2. Ps 88:4-9 NRSV. Verse 7 is omitted.

3. Bertolt Brecht, *Gesammelte Werke* 12, 466. Our translation.

4. The use of the intimate "*Du*" in the context of this oral presentation at the German Kirchentag implies an audience of Christian faith. It would be uncharacteristic of Soelle to presume an audience of Christians in other contexts.

5. The lines "a fairy tale from olden days / you can get it out of your head real fast" allude ironically to the German legend and folk song "Lorelei": "ein Märchen aus uralten Zeiten, das kommt mir nicht aus dem Sinn" (a fairy tale from olden days, I can't get it out of my head).

about the author

DOROTHEE SOELLE, BORN IN 1929 in Cologne, Germany, was a pioneer figure in feminist political theology of the late twentieth century and a widely published and translated poet and essayist, public speaker, peace activist, wife, mother, and grandmother. After studies in theology, she received a doctorate in literary criticism in 1954 and her second doctorate (habilitation) in philosophy in 1971, after her fourth child was born. From 1968 to 1972 she was active in an ecumenical "political even-song" group in Cologne combining reflection, prayer, and action on issues such as the Vietnam War and the arms race. She traveled and spoke widely in Europe, Asia, North America, and South America and facilitated discourse among liberation movements in these diverse contexts. In 1975 she relocated from Hamburg to New York and taught at Union Theological Seminary until 1987. She was a leading voice in ecumenical fora in Germany and North America, but her views were often contested by the established churches and no German theological faculty ever offered her a teaching posi-tion—according to Bishop Bärbel Wartenberg-Potter "one of the most remarkable blunders in post–World War II church history." Soelle died on April 27, 2003. Among her most influential works in English are *Christ the Representative* (1967), *Suffering* (1975), *Death by Bread Alone* (1978), *To Work and to Love* (1984), *Theology for Skeptics* (1994), *Against the Wind* (1999), and *The Silent Cry: Mysticism and Resistance* (2001).

about the translators

NANCY LUKENS-RUMSCHEIDT, BORN IN Washington, D.C., in 1945, is Professor of German and Women's Studies at the University of New Hampshire, teaching language, literature, and cultural studies. Her translations of German literature and theology include *Daughters of Eve: Women Writers from the German Democratic Republic* (1993), Dietrich Bonheoffer's *Sanctorum Communio: A Theological Study of the Sociology of the Church* (1998), and Dietrich Bonhoeffer's *Fiction from Tegel Prison* (2000). She is a member of Dover (N.H.) Friends Meeting (Quaker).

MARTIN LUKENS-RUMSCHEIDT, BORN IN Germany in 1935, is an ordained pastor in the United Church of Canada and was Professor of Systematic Theology at Atlantic School of Theology, Halifax, Nova Scotia, until his retirement. His publications include books on Karl Barth and Adolf von Harnack and essays on German theology, including one on the poetics of Dorothee Soelle. He is translator of Dietrich Bonhoeffer's *Act and Being* (*Dietrich Bonhoeffer Works*, English edition, vol. 2 [1996]) and co-translator with the late Barbara Rumscheidt of Soelle's *Against the Wind: Memoir of a Radical Christian* (1999), *The Silent Cry: Mysticism and Resistance* (2001), and three of her late essays in *The Theology of Dorothee Soelle* (ed. Sarah Pinnock, 2003).